CLASSIC DESSERT FOR TWO

CLASSIC DESSERT FOR TWO

Small-Batch Treats

NEW AND SELECTED RECIPES

CHRISTINA LANE

Countryman Press

An Imprint of W. W. Norton & Company
Independent Publishers Since 1923

For information about permission to reproduce selections from this book, write to Permissions, Countryman Press, 500 Fifth Avenue, New York, NY 10110

For information about special discounts for bulk purchases, please contact W. W. Norton Special Sales at specialsales@wwnorton.com or 800-233-4830

Manufacturing by Versa Press
Production manager: Devon Zahn

Countryman Press
www.countrymanpress.com

An imprint of W. W. Norton & Company, Inc.
500 Fifth Avenue, New York, NY 10110
www.wwnorton.com

978-1-68268-520-4

10 9 8 7 6 5 4 3 2 1

For the bakers. We work with butter, sugar, flour, and a prayer.

May we know how much those that eat our desserts appreciate us filling their bellies.

CONTENTS

INTRODUCTION

H I THERE! I hope we've met on my website or through one of my previous books but, if not, I am Christina Lane. I started scaling down dessert recipes when I was in graduate school and far from my family. I was craving the sort of sweet snacks that my grandmother would make for me when I was a child, hoping they would make me feel less homesick. The recipes were for full-sized treats, though, like Texas white sheet cake, fresh peach cobbler, and dozens of chocolate chip cookies. Too often, I wound up eating all the dessert. So I got out my measuring cups and started experimenting.

Baking is a science. You can't just cut your ingredients in half (or more) across the board. You have to consider the size of the pan, how the oven temperature might change, and whether you still need the same amount of baking powder or not. It sounds complicated, but I've done the work for you in these recipes. Little by little, I made progress. I figured out the best butter-to-egg-to-flour ratio to make a cake on a quarter sheet pan. A smaller cheesecake baked in a loaf pan was as flavorful as a full-sized one. Chocolate cream pie in a mason jar top was a revelation.

Since those days, and after writing four cookbooks based on that premise, I realized another reason why my followers love baking on this scale. Baking small-batch desserts can be the gateway to falling in love with baking. Starting with fewer ingredients and smaller batches makes baking less intimidating. Even if you have a total baking failure (which I highly doubt you will), you didn't waste too many ingredients, so you can simply rinse the bowls and try again.

Baking a small sheet of just six cookies is an approachable afternoon project that could lead to much more frequent and serious baking. Start with the small-batch cookies and explore around from there.

This is truly a collection of my favorite recipes, gathered together from my previous cookbooks, with twenty brand-new desserts to round out what I'm thinking of as my ultimate classic collection. If I could, I would bake and serve these to you in my own kitchen. I hope you're already subscribed to my website and can live vicariously through my videos. Please add comments and make suggestions.

EQUIPMENT
YOU WILL NEED

To make dessert for two, you may find you need some special equipment. Please don't feel as though you have to go out and buy every shape and size pan I use. Try to use what you have and if an alternative size other than the one I have listed works for you, great!

You've heard it before, but it bears repeating: Baking is a science. Measuring ingredients precisely is essential for success. This is even more pivotal in small-batch baking. One-eighth of a teaspoon might seem like nothing, but it is imperative to be precise.

MEASURING

MEASURING CUPS

You will need a set of measuring cups that range from ¼ cup to 1 full cup. Measuring cups are only for measuring dry ingredients, like flour and sugars. The best way to use a measuring cup is to fluff well the ingredient you plan to measure before you scoop it. Gently scoop the cup to overfill it, and then level the surface with a knife. Never pack ingredients into a measuring cup, unless it's brown sugar.

MEASURING SPOONS

You will need a set of measuring spoons that goes down to $1/8$ teaspoon. If it also has $3/4$ teaspoon, even better. These will be getting a lot of use in your kitchen.

GLASS MEASURING CUP

This is what you measure liquids in. Not for dry ingredients.

BAKEWARE

6-INCH PIE PAN

A 6- to 7-inch pie pan works great for my mini pie recipes. Typically, a 6-inch pie pan will measure 6 inches in diameter on the bottom but will flare out to 7 inches on top. I prefer an oven-safe glass pie pan so I can monitor the browning of the crust. The glass one in this book is my grandmother's, and I love it dearly.

6-INCH ROUND CAKE PAN

Essential for mini cakes. This pan is easy to find at craft or hobby stores, because it's technically the top layer of a wedding cake. Ideally, you want a 6-inch round cake pan that has 2-inch sides. If you use a pan that is deeper, your cake might sink when cooling.

4½-INCH AND 6-INCH ROUND MINI SPRINGFORM PAN

Makes the most adorable mini cheesecakes.

6-INCH CAST-IRON SKILLET
Did you know they made miniature cast-iron skillets? They're adorable!

BREAD LOAF PAN
A standard bread loaf pan that measures 9 by 5 by 3 inches is what we'll use to perfectly portion bars and even some pies.

RAMEKINS
I'm a bit of a ramekin fanatic. I collect them in every size, shape, and color. For the purposes of this book, you only need two sizes: the standard 6-ounce cup (the common size for crème brûlée) and the 10-ounce cup.

MINI GRATIN DISHES
I use smaller versions of gratin dishes to make cobblers, bread pudding, and crisps. My favorite is an 8-inch oval that holds 4 cups of water to the brim. Typically, the things we bake in these dishes are forgiving, as long as you keep an eye on them in the oven, so use whatever size small dishes you can find.

MUFFIN PANS
We may not fill every divot in the muffin pan, but we will make a small batch of cupcakes, mini cakes, and cookies! I rely on a standard muffin pan for such recipes as my S'mores Baked Alaska and Mini Raspberry Pies, and a mini muffin pan for Pumpkin Donut Holes and Frozen Margarita Tarts.

PETITE UTENSILS
Small utensils are not required for baking desserts for two, but I have a feeling the moment you try to wield a mini piece of pie from a mini pie dish with a regular-size pie server, you'll wish you had smaller tools. Here are a few of my favorite tiny utensils.

MINI WHISK
A mini whisk fits well in your hand and will whip a small amount of cream in no time.

MINI WOODEN SPOONS
In my opinion, you can never have enough wooden spoons in the kitchen. I use a small one for stirring homemade puddings and custards.

SMALL SPATULAS
I'm a firm believer in silicone spatulas. They help you get every last drop of batter from the bowl into the pan—very important when baking in small quantities. I use the mini ones intended for jam jars, but they're great for baking.

SMALL PIE SERVER
You'll need this for mini pies. Enough said.

PASTRY BRUSH
I brush all of my piecrusts with beaten egg yolk. It helps the crust turn golden brown, and it'll make your pies look as if they came from a bakery.

MINI MICROPLANE
There was a time when I thought Microplanes were extravagant. Now, I panic when I'm cooking in a kitchen without one. I use it for freshly grated nutmeg and citrus zest.

OTHER TOOLS
ELECTRIC MIXER
A large stand mixer is overkill for dessert for two—the paddle would spin without touching the small amount of batter. For this reason, I use a handheld electric mixer exclusively. I've used the same one for years, and it's never let me down.

MIXING BOWLS

If you buy a set of mixing bowls, you will only need the small and medium bowls for dessert for two. (Use the large bowl for salad to balance all the desserts you'll be eating.)

COLANDER/STRAINER

A small colander will help you rinse berries and sift flour or powdered sugar.

CULINARY TORCH

Oh, the things we will torch, you and I! I bought my torch for crème brûlée originally, but I find myself using it to crisp up bread pudding, leftover piecrust, and more.

SILICONE BAKING MATS

I use these instead of greasing my cookie sheet. I love that they're reusable, and nothing, I mean nothing, will stick to these.

PARCHMENT PAPER

I rely on parchment paper in cases where I can't use a silicone baking mat. While the brown paper gives my desserts the rustic vibe that I love, it really is a workhorse. Nothing sticks to parchment paper, not even tape (I tried it for photography purposes!). If you don't want to use parchment paper, grease your pans very well. When it comes to cakes, grease and flour the pans.

THE BAKING GOSPEL
(and Other Notes)

If someone asks for your recipe, share it. It's better to be known as the person who shares recipes than the person everyone must beg to make that cake one more time.

Cupcakes made with oil are always more tender than those made with butter (unless sour cream is involved). Save the butter for the frosting—and pile it on!

While we're talking about cupcakes . . . I always bake a small batch of cupcakes in the cups along the edge of the pan. I noticed they rise higher than the cups in the middle.

Creaming ingredients together is important. Blending the sugar into the fat in a recipe is a chance to dissolve the sugar, aerate the fat, and otherwise distribute flavors. Don't skimp. Let it be fluffy!

I'm always going to ask you to line your loaf pan with parchment paper, for easier removal of the baked loaf. The truth is, it can be tricky to wield a spatula in such a small pan. If you line with enough parchment to overhang, it serves as handles to lift out the dessert after baking.

Sweetened condensed milk. Let's face it: This stuff is sent from heaven. But desserts for two often only require a few tablespoons instead of the entire can. What to do? Buy the sweetened condensed milk sold in a squeeze bottle. I can always find it in the international aisle of even the smallest grocery stores.

A final note about ingredients: I recommend buying high-quality ingredients with which to bake. This is especially true for such things as cocoa powder and chocolate. For my recipe testing, I used name-brand ingredients. I'm not willing to take a risk with a dessert not turning out because of a store-brand product that contains water or cheap ingredients as filler. Use whatever you are comfortable with, but if your sour cream has the consistency of yogurt instead of thick cream, well, that's not right. The higher the fat content of your cocoa powder, the happier you'll be in life. Tested and proven.

COOKIES
&
BARS

Lavender Cookies

Sweet, chewy, and delicately floral cookies made with lavender buds are the latest cookie jar favorite in my house. These lavender cookies have chewy centers and barely crisp edges. They're nothing like shortbread cookies; they're a classic sugar cookie punctuated with the incredible scent and flavor of lavender buds. You can use lavender buds from your backyard garden (just make sure they haven't been sprayed with any chemicals) or you can pick up culinary dried lavender buds at the store. If you love the relaxing scent of lavender and enjoy the delicate flavor, you have to make these cookies!

YIELD · 6 COOKIES

4 tablespoons (½ stick) unsalted butter, melted

⅓ cup granulated sugar

½ teaspoon culinary-grade lavender buds

1 large egg yolk

½ teaspoon vanilla extract

¾ cup all-purpose flour

¼ teaspoon baking soda

⅛ teaspoon fine sea salt

Preheat the oven to 350°F and line a small baking sheet with parchment paper or a silicone mat.

Place the butter in a microwave-safe bowl and melt it in the microwave in 25-second intervals until fully melted. Keep an eye on it because if it gets too hot, it will splatter.

In a small food processor, combine the sugar and lavender buds and pulse a few times to break the buds into small pieces. Cover the food processor while you pulse so the sugar doesn't fly out.

Stir together the melted butter, lavender sugar, egg yolk, and vanilla extract. Stir very well to combine.

Next, sprinkle the flour, baking soda, and salt evenly over the dough, and stir just to combine.

Press the dough flat and evenly in the bowl, and then divide it in half by eye. You should get three cookies from each half.

Evenly space the cookies on the prepared baking sheet.

Bake for 10 minutes, until the cookies spread, start to crackle, and appear dry on top.

Let the cookies rest on the baking sheet for 2 minutes before moving them to a wire rack to cool completely.

Orange Cardamom Cookies

If you're looking to bake something full of winter spices, this is the place to start. These chewy Orange Cardamom Cookies remind me of those soft, spicy molasses cookies we all love around the holidays, but there are even more spices here. The orange zest makes them something unique and fresh. You will love their soft, chewy texture, similar to a bakery-style ginger cookie!

YIELD • 18 COOKIES

12 tablespoons (1½ sticks) unsalted butter, softened

1 cup brown sugar

2 tablespoons orange zest (from about 2 oranges)

1 large egg

¼ cup molasses

1 teaspoon vanilla extract

2¼ cups all-purpose flour

2 teaspoons baking soda

¼ teaspoon salt

2 teaspoons ground cardamom

⅓ cup granulated sugar, for rolling

In a large mixing bowl, using an electric mixer on medium speed, beat the butter until smooth and creamy.

Beat in the brown sugar and orange zest until just combined.

Beat in the egg, scraping the bowl. Beat in the molasses and vanilla.

Carefully, sprinkle the flour, baking soda, salt, and cardamom evenly over the surface of the dough, and then beat until just combined.

Refrigerate the dough for at least 2 hours to firm it up.

Preheat the oven to 350°F. Line a baking sheet with parchment paper. Scoop out large (about 2-tablespoon) chunk of dough and roll lightly in your hands to form a ball.

Roll each cookie in the granulated sugar, and then place them evenly spaced apart on the prepared baking sheet. You will only be able to fit 12 cookies on a sheet; just refrigerate the remaining dough and repeat the process until all of the dough is used up. Bake for 11 to 13 minutes, or just until the edges set. Let cool on the baking sheet for a few minutes before moving to a wire rack to cool completely.

Brownie Cookies

You know these cookies. They are big, crispy, crunchy, and chewy all at once. They are positively cravable in a way that no other cookie is. Lucky for you, I scaled them down so you can have damage control taken care of before you even start eating!

YIELD · 10 COOKIES

2 large egg whites

¼ teaspoon vanilla extract

1 cup powdered sugar

⅓ cup unsweetened cocoa powder

⅛ teaspoon salt

3 tablespoons chocolate chips

Preheat the oven to 350°F and line a baking sheet with a silicone mat or parchment paper.

In a medium bowl, using an electric mixer on high speed, beat the egg whites and vanilla until soft peaks form.

In a separate bowl, whisk together the powdered sugar, cocoa powder, and salt. Ensure the mixture is free of lumps.

Add half of the dry ingredients to the egg white mixture and fold until no streaks remain. Fold in the remaining dry ingredients, and finally stir in the chocolate chips.

Scoop 10 equal portions of batter onto the prepared baking sheet. Use two cookie sheets because these cookies spread quite a bit.

Bake the cookies for 15 to 17 minutes. The surface of the cookies will appear dry and they will start to crack around the edges.

Let cool on the baking sheet for a few minutes before moving to a cooling rack.

Chocolate Sugar Cookies
with Raspberry Curd

These chocolate sugar cookies are everything a sugar cookie should be: soft, chewy, sparkling with sugar, and perfect for smashing raspberry curd between. If you don't have time to make the raspberry curd, it's fine—the cookies stand on their own just as well. These cookies are messy to eat with the raspberry curd, but oh so good!

YIELD • 4 SANDWICH COOKIES

FOR THE COOKIES
4 tablespoons (½ stick) unsalted butter, at room temperature

¼ cup + 2 tablespoons light brown sugar

1 large egg yolk

¼ teaspoon vanilla extract

3 tablespoons unsweetened cocoa powder

½ cup all-purpose flour

¼ teaspoon baking soda

¼ teaspoon salt

2 tablespoons granulated sugar, for rolling

TO MAKE THE COOKIES: In a medium bowl, using an electric mixer on medium speed, beat the butter until fluffy, about 1 minute. Add the brown sugar and beat for another minute. Next, add the egg yolk and vanilla and beat until well combined.

In a separate bowl, whisk together the cocoa powder, flour, baking soda, and salt until no lumps remain. Add the dry ingredients to the wet ingredients in two increments, mixing between each addition. Cover the dough and chill it for at least 1 hour. The dough can be made in advance or even frozen.

When ready to bake, preheat the oven to 350°F. Line a cookie sheet with parchment paper.

Place the granulated sugar in a shallow bowl.

Scoop eight equal portions of dough, roll them in your hand to form perfect balls, and then roll through the sugar to coat. Space evenly apart on the prepared cookie sheet.

Bake for 8 to 10 minutes, until set in the center and beginning to crackle.

Let cool completely on the cookie sheet.

FOR THE RASPBERRY CURD

4 tablespoons (½ stick) unsalted butter

6 ounces raspberries (frozen is fine)

Juice from 1 small lemon

¼ cup + 2 tablespoons granulated sugar

⅛ teaspoon salt

3 large egg yolks

¼ teaspoon vanilla extract

TO MAKE THE RASPBERRY CURD: In a medium saucepan, melt the butter over medium heat. Add the raspberries, lemon juice, sugar, and salt. Bring to a simmer over medium-high heat, stirring occasionally. There should be tiny bubbles along the edges of the pan.

Place the egg yolks in a small bowl on the side. Add a small scoop of the simmering raspberry mixture to the egg yolks and stir vigorously. Repeat a few times. Then, pour the entire egg yolk mixture back into the saucepan and bring to a brisk simmer over medium-high heat, stirring occasionally. Cook for 1 minute, then remove from the heat and stir in the vanilla. Pour the raspberry mixture into a bowl, press plastic wrap directly on the surface, and refrigerate for at least 4 hours.

To serve, scoop the raspberry curd onto four of the cookies. Top with the remaining four cookies to make messy, delicious sandwiches.

Beer Brownies

An excellent contender for a Valentine's Day gift or dessert! While these are a tad more work than regular brownies, boiling beer on the stove until it reduces to a syrup is the best flavor enhancement possible for warm, chocolatey brownies. You'll use the beer syrup in the brownies and a little in the frosting, too. Only use the optional unsweetened chocolate if you like fudgy brownies; omit it if you prefer more cake-y brownies.

YIELD • 2 GENEROUS SERVINGS

FOR THE BEER BROWNIES

1 cup dark beer (I used coffee stout)

8 tablespoons (1 stick) unsalted butter

½ cup + 1 tablespoon unsweetened cocoa powder

1 cup + 2 tablespoons granulated sugar

2 ounces unsweetened chocolate, chopped (optional)

1 large egg white

1 teaspoon vanilla extract

¼ teaspoon fine sea salt

½ cup all-purpose flour

FOR THE FROSTING

6 tablespoons (¾ stick) unsalted butter, softened

1 cup powdered sugar

FIRST, MAKE THE BEER CONCENTRATE: Add the beer to a small saucepan and boil until it reduces to ⅓ cup. It will take about 20 minutes. Keep an eye on it to prevent it from boiling over.

Preheat the oven to 325°F and line a loaf pan with parchment paper.

In a microwave-safe bowl, combine the butter, cocoa powder, sugar, and unsweetened chocolate (if using). Microwave at full power for 30 seconds. Stir, then microwave for another 30 seconds. Let the mixture cool for 1 minute.

Stir in 4 tablespoons of the beer concentrate, the egg white, vanilla, and salt.

Finally, mix in the flour and stir for 50 strokes to incorporate and activate the gluten in the flour.

Pour the mixture into the loaf pan and bake for 40 to 45 minutes. It's done when the surface is dry and an inserted toothpick has only moist crumbs sticking to it. Let cool.

Once the brownies are cool, make the frosting: beat together the softened butter and powdered sugar until combined.

Beat in the remaining beer concentrate (1 tablespoon).

Frost the brownies and serve.

Orange Chocolate Chunk Cookies

It's not that standard chocolate chip cookies needed to be improved upon; it's that I love the combination of orange and chocolate! With a packed ½ teaspoon of orange zest, these cookies really sing with flavor.

YIELD · 12 COOKIES

6 tablespoons (¾ stick) unsalted butter, softened

¼ cup dark brown sugar, packed

3 tablespoons granulated sugar

1 large egg yolk

½ teaspoon vanilla extract

½ teaspoon freshly grated orange zest

½ cup + 2 tablespoons all-purpose flour

⅛ teaspoon fine sea salt

¼ teaspoon baking soda

¼ teaspoon baking powder

⅓ cup chocolate chunks

Preheat the oven to 375°F and line a baking sheet with parchment paper or a silicone mat.

In a medium bowl, add the butter and beat on medium speed with an electric mixer. Beat for just a few seconds to break it up and make it lightly fluffy, about 10 seconds.

Add the brown sugar and granulated sugar to the butter and beat until fluffy, about 45 seconds.

Next, add the egg yolk, vanilla, and orange zest to the bowl, and beat until combined.

Evenly sprinkle the flour, salt, baking soda, and baking powder on top, and beat until just combined—do not overmix.

Finally, stir in the chocolate chunks by hand. Scrape the bottom of the bowl well to ensure all of the flour is incorporated.

Divide the dough into 12 balls and space them evenly on the prepared baking sheet.

Bake for 8 minutes and check them—the cookies should be golden on the edges. If not, return to the oven for up to 2 more minutes, but be careful not to overbake or they will lose their chewy centers.

Let the cookies cool on the sheet pan for 1 minute before moving to a wire rack to cool completely before serving.

Who am I kidding? Eat these babies warm!

Pumpkin Spice Palmiers

A four-ingredient cookie that you will find irresistible! These palmiers are also known as elephant ear cookies, but I adore their heart-shape, so I call them heart cookies. Buttery puff pastry rolled up while being enrobed in sugar produces these flaky, caramelized little cookies. The pumpkin spice makes them perfect for fall, too!

YIELD • 16 COOKIES

1 sheet frozen puff pastry

1 cup sugar

½ teaspoon fine sea salt

½ teaspoon pumpkin pie spice

Thaw the puff pastry overnight in the fridge, or on the counter at room temperature for 30 minutes. It should be pliable and soft before using, not cracking around the edges.

In a small bowl, whisk together the sugar, salt, and pumpkin pie spice until evenly blended.

On a flat surface for rolling, sprinkle a little less than half of the sugar mixture. Unroll the puff pastry sheet and place it on top of the sugar. Roll the pastry out to a 13-inch square.

Sprinkle another handful of the sugar mixture on top of the square. Use a rolling pin to press the sugar into the dough.

Start the folds: Take the right and left edge of the dough and fold in half, inward toward the center.

Sprinkle more sugar on top. Fold the outside edges inward again, toward the center.

Finally, fold the entire dough in half like a book by folding and stacking the left side over the right side. This will make a log. Sprinkle with the remaining sugar and gently press into the dough. There will be some excess sugar on the board.

Place the dough on the parchment-lined baking sheet and place it in the fridge for 30 minutes.

Meanwhile, preheat the oven to 450°F.

After the 30 minutes, slice the cookies into ¾-inch slices and space them at least 3 inches apart on a baking sheet.

Bake the cookies for 6 minutes, then quickly flip them with a metal spatula, and bake them for another 3 to 5 minutes, until they're golden brown and caramelized on both sides.

Let the palmiers rest on the sheet for a few minutes, and then let them cool completely on a wire rack. They will crisp as they cool.

Mini Moon Pies

I call these "quick" moon pies, because the only thing we're making from scratch is the cookie dough. And really, it's so easy, just a small batch of shortbread dough that has honey for sweetness and crispness. The honey also lends the graham cracker—like taste that moon pies have. Once the cookies are done, we're going to spread on marshmallow cream (yes, straight from the jar!), dunk them in chocolate, and then devour.

You can dunk the cookies entirely in chocolate for more authentic moon pies. The recipe accounts for plenty of extra chocolate for double dipping, too!

YIELD • 6 MINI MOON PIES

FOR THE DOUGH
4 tablespoons (½ stick) unsalted butter, softened

¼ cup powdered sugar

1 tablespoon honey

½ teaspoon vanilla extract

½ cup all-purpose flour, plus extra for rolling

¼ teaspoon fine sea salt

FOR ASSEMBLING MOON PIES
About ¼ cup marshmallow fluff

1 cup chocolate chips

1 tablespoon coconut oil

Preheat the oven to 350°F and line a baking sheet with parchment paper or a silicone mat.

In a medium bowl, add the butter, powdered sugar, honey, and vanilla. Beat the mixture on medium speed with an electric mixer until light and fluffy.

Next, sprinkle the flour and salt evenly on top. Beat together until just combined.

Cover the bowl and refrigerate the dough for 30 minutes.

Next, heavily flour a board. Place the cookie dough on top and sprinkle more flour on top of the dough. Use your fingers to press the dough out into a rough 6-inch square, using lots of flour as you go.

Using a 2-inch-wide biscuit cutter that you dip in flour, cut out 12 circles from the dough. Use a spatula to carefully move the dough circles to the baking sheet.

Bake for 10 minutes, or until the edges of the cookies start to turn golden brown.

Let cookies cool completely, leaving them on the baking sheet.

Meanwhile, melt the chocolate chips and coconut oil in a double boiler. Alternatively, set a microwave to 50 percent power and heat the chocolate chips and coconut oil in 30-second pulses, stirring between each pulse, until melted and smooth.

Spread a scant teaspoon of marshmallow filling on top of six cookies. Press the remaining cookies on top, dunk in the melted chocolate, and place on a wax paper—lined plate to chill in the fridge for a few minutes before serving.

These cookies keep in the fridge for a few days or tightly wrapped in the freezer for your next moon pie craving. The longer the sandwiches sit, the softer the cookies become (and more authentic to the original moon pies, too!).

Chocolate Ice Cream Sandwiches

May I suggest something a little less expected on Valentine's Day? Sure, a warm chocolate dessert is always good. But I think a chewy chocolate cookie stuffed with strawberry ice cream is even better. It's not Valentine's Day without chocolate and strawberries, and this fun spin on that flavor combo is all I want from my valentine!

**YIELD · 4 COOKIE
SANDWICHES**

**1 pint store-bought
strawberry ice cream**

¾ cup all-purpose flour

**3 tablespoons unsweetened
cocoa powder**

Pinch of fine sea salt

**4 tablespoons (½ stick)
unsalted butter, softened**

⅔ cup powdered sugar

2 tablespoons dark brown sugar

1¼ teaspoons vanilla extract

1 large egg yolk

2 tablespoons molasses

**2 tablespoons granulated
sugar, for flattening cookies**

Let the ice cream soften at room temperature for about 15 minutes.

When the ice cream is soft, scoop all of it out of the carton and into an 8-inch square brownie pan. Press it as flat as possible. Place it back in the freezer for at least 15 minutes.

Then, make the cookies: preheat the oven to 350°F and line a baking sheet with parchment paper or a silicone mat.

Whisk together the flour, cocoa, and salt. Set aside.

In a separate bowl, beat the butter, powdered sugar, brown sugar, and vanilla until fluffy.

Finally, beat in the egg yolk and molasses.

Add the dry ingredients to the wet in three batches and beat until just combined. Divide the dough in half by eye, and make four dough scoops out of each. Roll the dough in your hands to make eight balls and space them evenly on the baking sheet. Dip the bottom of a small glass in the granulated sugar and lightly press the cookies flat.

Bake for 10 minutes.

When the cookies have cooled, use a 3-inch cookie or biscuit cutter (about the same size as the cookies) to cut out four perfect "slices" of ice cream.

Place each slice of ice cream between two cookies and serve immediately, or wrap in plastic wrap and freeze, then rest them on the counter for 5 minutes before serving.

Just One Chocolate Chip Cookie

If you've ever wanted to make a single-serve cookie to enjoy alone, I have the recipe for you! My recipe for Just One Chocolate Chip Cookie has been perfected over years: after tweaking teaspoons of sugar and butter for ages, I finally landed on the right combination. It's chewy in the center and slightly crisp on the edges, which is the exact definition of perfection. Save this recipe for rainy days and TV binge nights!

YIELD · 1 COOKIE

2 tablespoons unsalted butter, melted

3 tablespoons brown sugar

1 egg yolk

¼ teaspoon vanilla extract

¼ cup + 2 teaspoons all-purpose flour

⅛ teaspoon fine sea salt

2 tablespoons chocolate chips, plus more for topping

Flaky sea salt, for topping (optional)

Preheat the oven to 350°F and line a small cookie sheet with parchment paper.

In a small bowl, combine the melted butter and brown sugar. Mix the butter and brown sugar together with a small spatula.

Next, add the egg yolk and vanilla and mix well.

Then, sprinkle the flour and salt evenly over the bowl, and stir until just combined.

Finally, sprinkle in the chocolate chips.

Scoop the cookie dough onto the cookie sheet and try to mound it up a bit. Place a few more chocolate chips on top. Sprinkle with flaky sea salt, if using.

Bake for 14 to 16 minutes. The cookie is done when the edges are turning golden brown, but the center may stay a bit gooey and soft. Let the cookie cool completely on the pan so that it sets.

Double Chocolate Chip Cookies

Sometimes, a chocolate chip cookie isn't enough. You need even more chocolate. Actually, I need even more chocolate. These chocolate cookies are studded with big chocolate chunks and sprinkled with salt before serving. They're every bit as dreamy as they sound.

YIELD • 9 OR 10 COOKIES

4 tablespoons (½ stick) unsalted butter, at room temperature

¼ cup + 2 tablespoons packed light brown sugar

1 large egg yolk

½ teaspoon vanilla extract

3 tablespoons unsweetened cocoa powder

½ cup all-purpose flour

¼ teaspoon instant espresso powder

¼ teaspoon baking soda

¼ teaspoon salt

¼ cup (heaping) chocolate chunks

A pinch of large-grained salt, for sprinkling (optional)

In a medium bowl, beat the butter with an electric mixer on high speed until fluffy, about 1 minute. Add the brown sugar and beat for another minute. Add the egg yolk and vanilla and beat until well combined.

In a separate bowl, whisk together the cocoa powder, flour, espresso powder, baking soda, and salt until no lumps remain.

Add the dry ingredients to the wet ingredients in two increments, mixing between each addition. Finally, stir in the chocolate chunks.

Cover the dough and chill it for at least 1 hour. The dough can be made in advance or even frozen.

When ready to bake, preheat the oven to 350°F. Spray a cookie sheet with cooking spray or line it with parchment paper.

Scoop out 9 or 10 equal portions of dough and roll each in your hands to form a ball. Place each cookie at least 1 inch apart on the prepared cookie sheet.

Bake for 8 to 10 minutes. Check the cookies after 8 minutes—if the edges are set, remove from the oven and let cool for 5 minutes on the baking sheet before moving to a wire rack to cool completely.

Small-Batch Espresso Chocolate Chip Cookies

In our search for a chocolate chip cookie "house recipe," we've been through a lot of butter and chocolate chips.

This recipe is nearly a decade in the making, and it's finally perfect. I add an indecent amount of espresso powder and a heavy pinch of salt. They're addicting!

YIELD · 12 SMALL COOKIES

6 tablespoons (¾ stick) salted butter

¼ cup dark brown sugar

3 tablespoons granulated sugar

1 large egg yolk

½ vanilla bean, sliced open and scraped

½ cup plus 2 tablespoons all-purpose flour

¼ teaspoon fine sea salt

1 heaping teaspoon instant espresso powder

¼ teaspoon baking soda

¼ teaspoon baking powder

⅓ cup semisweet chocolate chips

Flaky sea salt, for topping (optional)

Preheat the oven to 375°F. Line a baking sheet with a silicone mat.

In a medium bowl, beat the butter with an electric mixer on medium speed until it's fluffy, about 20 seconds.

Add both sugars and beat for another 30 seconds. The mixture will turn a pale color and be fluffy.

Next, add the egg yolk and the insides from the vanilla bean and beat until they're just combined.

Whisk together the flour, salt, espresso powder, baking soda, and baking powder in a separate bowl.

Sprinkle the flour mixture on top of the butter mixture and beat just until they're combined.

Stir in the chocolate chips.

Scoop the dough into 12 dough balls and space them evenly on the baking sheet. Sprinkle with flaky sea salt, if using.

Bake for 8 to 10 minutes, removing the cookies from the oven when the edges just start to turn golden brown.

Let the cookies rest on the baking sheet for 1 minute before moving them to a wire rack to cool.

Lemon Shortbread Cookies

As if anything cut into a heart shape could get any cuter, I decorate these Lemon Shortbread Cookies with a drizzle of tangy lemon icing and fresh lemon zest. These are perfect for Valentine's Day, Mother's Day, or any time you need a springtime treat!

YIELD · 18 COOKIES

FOR THE COOKIES
8 tablespoons (1 stick) unsalted butter, softened

¼ cup powdered sugar, plus more for rolling

½ tablespoon fresh lemon zest (from 2 lemons)

1 cup all-purpose flour, plus more for pan

¼ teaspoon salt

FOR THE LEMON GLAZE
1 tablespoon fresh lemon juice (from ½ lemon)

½ cup powdered sugar

Preheat the oven to 325°F. Line two baking sheets with parchment paper.

In a large bowl, add the butter and powdered sugar. Beat with an electric mixer on medium-high speed until fluffy, at least 2 minutes.

Add the lemon zest and beat again.

Sprinkle the flour and salt on top of the butter mixture and beat until just combined.

If the dough seems overly crumbly and dry, squeeze in a few drops of lemon juice at a time until it comes together.

Lightly dust a surface with powdered sugar. Gather half of the dough into a disk, and using a rolling pin dusted with powdered sugar, roll out the dough to slightly less than ½-inch thickness. These cookies should be somewhat thick for the best texture.

Use any cookie cutters you like to cut out shapes. Use a small spatula to move the cookies to the sheet pan. Repeat with remaining half of dough until all of the dough is used to make cookies. You will get about 18 cookies, depending on the size of your cookie cutter.

Bake for 9 minutes, until the edges of the cookies just start to turn a very light golden brown. Keep an eye on the cookie sheet on the bottom rack, and if your oven doesn't bake evenly, you may need to rotate the pans halfway through the baking time.

Let the cookies cool completely on the sheets.

Before serving, whisk together the lemon juice and powdered sugar until easily pourable. Drizzle the lemon glaze over the cookies and serve.

A Dozen Cut-Out Sugar Cookies

I love how all grocery stores in the country strategically place clear containers of frosted sugar cookies with sprinkles near the checkout aisle. I can't resist them. I love a good cut-out sugar cookie topped with frosting and sprinkles. This is your new go-to small-batch sugar cookie recipe. This recipe is for rolling and cutting out shapes—make these at the holidays with your favorite cookie cutters.

Oh, and you don't have to use Texas-shaped cookie cutters for this recipe, but your cookies won't be nearly as cute without it.

YIELD · 12 COOKIES

FOR THE COOKIES
¾ cup all-purpose flour, plus extra for rolling

½ teaspoon baking powder

Pinch of salt

4 tablespoons (½ stick) unsalted butter, at room temperature

¼ cup sugar

1 large egg yolk

½ teaspoon vanilla extract

⅛ teaspoon almond extract

TO MAKE THE COOKIES: Preheat the oven to 350°F and line a baking sheet with parchment paper or a silicone mat.

In a small bowl, whisk together the flour, baking powder, and salt. In a medium bowl, beat together with an electric mixer the butter and sugar. Once light and fluffy, beat in the egg yolk and extracts. Once they are well incorporated, sprinkle half of the flour mixture over the butter mixture and beat gently until combined, then sprinkle with the rest of the flour mixture. Beat until no streaks of flour remain, but be careful not to overmix.

Dust a clean countertop with flour, and dump the dough out onto it. Gather it into a ball and press it into a 2-inch-thick disk. Flour your rolling pin, then roll out the dough big enough to cut out about eight shapes with your choice of cookie cutter(s). Place the shapes on a baking sheet lined with parchment paper or a silicone mat. Gather the dough scraps and reroll to cut out four more shapes and place them on the cookie sheet.

Place the cookie sheet in the freezer for 5 minutes.

Bake the cookies for 10 to 12 minutes, until their edges just start to turn brown. Let them sit on the sheet a few minutes before moving them to a wire rack to cool completely.

FOR THE ICING

1½ cups powdered sugar

2 to 3 tablespoons milk

⅛ teaspoon vanilla extract

Sprinkles, for decorating

TO MAKE THE ICING: Once the cookies are completely cool, whisk together all the icing ingredients. Start with 1 tablespoon of milk and add up to 2 more tablespoons to achieve a slightly runny consistency. Ice your cookies by outlining the shape using a squeeze bottle or small piping bag with a tip, then flood the icing within the borders to fill it in. Top with sprinkles and enjoy!

Raspberry Brownies
with Chambord Glaze

If I'm picking a Valentine's Day dessert, it's going to be brownies. My brownies are baked in a loaf pan, and when cut down the middle after baking they make two perfectly portioned brownies. My brownies have an intense chocolate hit from unsweetened cocoa powder, plus a small amount of flour for chewiness.

Dollop raspberries on top of the batter before baking and drizzle these with a Chambord (raspberry liqueur) glaze for the best chocolate raspberry dessert you've ever had.

YIELD · 2 GENEROUS SERVINGS

FOR THE BROWNIES

5 tablespoons unsalted butter

½ cup plus 2 tablespoons granulated sugar

½ cup unsweetened cocoa powder

½ teaspoon vanilla extract

¼ teaspoon almond extract

¼ teaspoon salt

1 large egg

¼ cup all-purpose flour

Small handful fresh raspberries

FOR THE CHAMBORD GLAZE

½ cup powdered sugar

1 tablespoon Chambord (raspberry liqueur)

Preheat the oven to 325°F and make sure an oven rack is in the lower third of the oven.

Line a 9-by-5-inch loaf pan with parchment paper in two directions, overlapping; let the parchment paper overhang the sides to use as handles to lift out the brownies once they're baked.

Next, in a microwave-safe bowl, combine the butter, sugar, and cocoa powder.

Microwave for 30 seconds, stop and stir, and microwave for another 30 seconds. The mixture will be quite hot.

Let the mixture rest on the counter for a few minutes to cool, stirring occasionally.

When the mixture feels warm but not hot, stir in the vanilla, almond extract, and salt. Finally, stir in the egg.

Add the flour to the batter and, using a spatula, vigorously stir the mixture for 50 strokes. This activates the gluten and makes for rich, chewy brownies.

Spread the batter evenly into the prepared pan. Sprinkle the raspberries on top, pressing some into the batter.

Bake for 23 to 26 minutes, until the top is dry.

While the brownies cool, whisk together the glaze in a small bowl. Add more Chambord as needed to make a smooth glaze.

Drizzle the glaze over the brownies, cut them into pieces, and serve.

Snickerdoodles

There are some days when nothing but a crinkly cinnamon sugar cookie will do. This recipe uses cream cheese in the dough, for a bit of tang. You just may eat all 10 cookies by yourself!

YIELD · 10 COOKIES

3 tablespoons unsalted butter, at room temperature

2 ounces cream cheese, softened

½ cup + 2 tablespoons granulated sugar, divided

1 large egg

¾ cup + 2 tablespoons all-purpose flour

1 teaspoon cream of tartar

½ teaspoon baking soda

⅛ teaspoon salt

2 teaspoons ground cinnamon

Preheat the oven to 350°F and position a rack in the center of the oven. Line a cookie sheet with a silicone mat or parchment paper.

In a medium bowl, using an electric mixer on medium speed, beat the butter, cream cheese, and ½ cup of the sugar. Beat until well mixed and fluffy, about 1 minute. Next, beat in the egg.

In a small bowl, stir together the flour, cream of tartar, baking soda, and salt. Sprinkle this mixture over the butter mixture and beat until just combined.

In a shallow bowl, stir together the remaining 2 tablespoons of sugar and the cinnamon. Scoop a heaping tablespoon of the dough, roll it in your palm lightly, and then roll it in the cinnamon-sugar mixture to coat. Repeat with remaining dough. You should get 10 cookies.

Space the dough balls evenly apart on the prepared baking sheet, then bake for 10 to 12 minutes.

Let cool on the baking sheet for 1 minute, and then move to a cooling rack to cool completely.

Best-Ever Jam Bars

I can be a bit of a jam hoarder. It's one of my favorite things to buy at farmers' markets, and it's my favorite gift to receive. (Take note!)

A lot of jam bars are too soggy for me. It's just the nature of the beast—baking sugary jam in between layers of soft batter. But I fixed the problem for us! A little almond meal (just ground almonds—you can make it yourself in a food processor) and coconut flakes in the batter make for a jam bar with a crisp crust and a molten jam center.

I'm not even afraid to say it: these are the best jam bars ever.

YIELD · 6 BARS

½ cup almond meal

1 cup all-purpose flour

½ cup unsweetened coconut flakes

¼ teaspoon fine sea salt

¼ teaspoon baking powder

9 tablespoons unsalted butter, softened, plus extra for greasing the pan

¼ cup dark brown sugar

½ cup granulated sugar

1 large egg white

Heaping ½ cup of your favorite jam

Preheat the oven to 350°F and butter an 8-inch square baking dish.

In a medium bowl, whisk together the almond meal, flour, coconut, salt, and baking powder.

In a separate bowl, cream the softened butter with the sugars until light and fluffy. Add the egg white and beat until combined.

Add the dry ingredients to the wet and beat until combined.

Spread half of the dough onto the bottom of the baking dish, using your fingers to press it into an even layer.

Spread the jam over the surface (if you leave a half-centimeter border, the bars won't stick to the pan as badly).

Top the jam with the remaining dough, using your fingers to make big crumbles of dough.

Bake for 30 to 32 minutes, until the edges start to turn deeply golden brown.

Let cool in the pan, then cut and serve.

White Chocolate Raspberry Cookies

It's time to combine my favorite flavor combo into one incredibly easy, chewy bite. You will love these White Chocolate Raspberry Cookies right out of the oven! The dough can be made ahead of time, and refrigerated until you need it. You can also freeze raw dough or already baked cookies.

YIELD · 18 COOKIES

12 tablespoons (1½ sticks) unsalted butter, softened

½ cup brown sugar

¼ cup granulated sugar

1 large egg

1½ teaspoons vanilla extract

1½ cups all-purpose flour

¼ teaspoon salt

½ teaspoon baking soda

½ teaspoon baking powder

½ cup white chocolate chips, plus more for topping

½ cup fresh raspberries, plus more for topping

In a large mixing bowl, add the softened butter, brown sugar, and granulated sugar. Beat the butter and sugars together with an electric hand mixer on high speed, 2 to 3 minutes, until pale in color and fluffy.

Add the egg and vanilla and beat until combined.

Sprinkle the flour, salt, baking soda, and baking powder evenly over the bowl. Beat the dry ingredients into the wet ingredients.

Add the white chocolate and raspberries and fold in by hand. You want to smash some of the raspberries, but not all of them.

Refrigerate the dough for 1 hour. Do not skip this step!

Preheat the oven to 350°F. Line a baking sheet with parchment paper or a silicone mat.

Scoop out heaping tablespoon-sized dough balls and space them evenly on the prepared baking sheet.

Press extra white chocolate chips and one raspberry piece on the top of each cookie.

Bake for 11 to 13 minutes, until the edges start to turn golden brown. Don't underbake these cookies because the juice from the raspberries will make them too soft.

When the cookies come out of the oven, press a few more pieces of white chocolate on top.

Move to a cooling rack to cool completely before serving.

Blackberry Scone Cookies

These cookies are like a mash-up of strawberry shortcake: the tender not-too-sweet biscuit, the fresh berries, the crusty edges—it's all here.

My daughter's favorite combination is blackberries and coconut sugar, but feel free to mix it up and use strawberries and regular sugar. If you use strawberries, double the amount.

These cookies aren't too sweet, and that's exactly what I love about them. They're great for breakfast or an afternoon snack with a toddler who just woke up from a nap.

YIELD • 12 COOKIES

3 ounces fresh blackberries (a handful)

1 cup all-purpose flour

1 teaspoon baking powder

¼ teaspoon fine sea salt

⅓ cup coconut sugar

3 tablespoons cold unsalted butter

⅓ cup + 1 tablespoon heavy cream

Coarse sanding sugar for topping (optional)

First, preheat the oven to 350°F and line a baking sheet with parchment paper or a silicone mat.

Next, slice the blackberries in half or quarter them, depending on size.

In a medium bowl, combine the flour, baking powder, salt, and sugar. Stir with a fork until well blended.

Next, add the butter and cut it into the mixture using two knives or a pastry blender. Work the butter in until it's evenly dispersed and is smaller than peas.

Add the heavy cream and stir gently until a dough forms.

Sprinkle in the blackberries and fold gently to combine.

Scoop 12 balls of dough onto the baking sheet (or make six larger cookies) and top with a sprinkling of coarse sugar (if using). Bake the cookies for 20 to 25 minutes.

Immediately move the cookies to a wire rack to cool completely before serving. The cookies soften as they rest so they're best when served the same day.

Frozen Margarita Tarts

If I had to pick one thing to be the most proud about being a Texan, it would be the invention of the frozen margarita in my hometown of Dallas. It's the world's most perfect drink. When I go home to visit Dallas I subsist on a steady diet of chips, salsa, queso, guac, and frozen margaritas. Somehow, I feel like I'm hitting all the major food groups on this diet. Please don't correct me if I'm wrong!

I created a dessert inspired by my beloved frozen margarita. And since I never forget the salt rim on my frozen margarita, I used crushed pretzels as the crust for these tarts for the salty bite. Feel free to double, triple, even quadruple this recipe for your Cinco de Mayo festivities!

YIELD · 6 TARTS

FOR THE CRUST
1 cup mini pretzel twists

3 tablespoons unsalted butter, melted, plus more for greasing pan

FOR THE LIME CURD FILLING
¼ cup granulated sugar

1 large egg

3 tablespoons fresh lime juice

Zest of 1 small lime

1 tablespoon unsalted butter

1 drop green food coloring (optional)

3 tablespoons heavy whipping cream

2 teaspoons powdered sugar

1 teaspoon tequila

TO MAKE THE CRUST: Crush the pretzels in a food processor (or place in a plastic bag and use a rolling pin). You want a fine powder, but a few pieces of pretzels remaining are fine. Next, stir in the melted butter until combined.

Pack a heaping tablespoon of the pretzel crumbs into six well-greased cups of a mini muffin pan. You should have six tart crusts. Place in the freezer to set.

TO MAKE THE LIME CURD FILLING: In a microwave-safe bowl, combine the granulated sugar, egg, lime juice, butter, and food coloring, if using. Whisk together, then microwave on high for 30 seconds. Stop, stir, and microwave for another 30 seconds. Repeat until the mixture thickens and coats the back of a spoon. For me, this takes 1 minute and 30 seconds, or three pulses.

Scrape the filling into a shallow bowl (more surface area, faster cooling), press plastic wrap directly onto the surface, and refrigerate until cold, about 1 hour.

One hour before serving, dollop the filling over the frozen pretzel crusts. In a medium bowl, using an electric mixer on medium speed, whip the cream until soft peaks form, and then stir in the powdered sugar and tequila. Spoon the whipped cream on top of the lime curd, and freeze until set.

To serve, run a knife around the edge of the tarts, and pop each out onto a plate.

Lemon Meringue Pie Cookies

I am a lemon dessert lover. These cookies taste like a bite of lemon meringue pie, and I can't get enough of them. Make the meringue cookie shells, and fill them with whatever filling you like: chocolate pudding, vanilla pudding, or this lemon cream filling.

YIELD · 4 COOKIES

FOR THE MERINGUE
1 large egg white

⅛ teaspoon cream of tartar

¼ cup granulated sugar

FOR THE LEMON CURD
2 tablespoons unsalted butter, at room temperature

¼ cup granulated sugar

1 large egg + 2 large egg yolks

⅓ cup fresh lemon juice

Pinch of salt

¼ cup heavy whipping cream

1 tablespoon powdered sugar

TO MAKE THE MERINGUE: First, preheat the oven to 200°F. Line a small sheet pan with parchment paper or a silicone mat.

In a medium bowl, using an electric mixer on medium speed, beat the egg white and cream of tartar until soft peaks form. Then, slowly stream in the sugar while beating. Beat until the mixture has stiff peaks.

Using two spoons or a piping bag, make four equal disks about 4 inches in diameter of the meringue mixture on the prepared sheet pan.

Bake for 40 minutes, and then turn off the oven and let the meringues cool inside the oven for 1 hour. Do not open the oven door.

TO MAKE THE LEMON CURD: In a medium bowl, using an electric mixer on high speed, beat together the butter and sugar until well combined. Add the egg and egg yolks one at a time while beating constantly. Finally, stream in the lemon juice and salt. The mixture may look a bit curdled—it's fine.

Pour the lemon curd into a small saucepan and bring to a simmer over medium-low heat to thicken. Stir constantly to avoid burning. Once simmering, remove from the heat and let cool.

In a separate medium bowl, using an electric mixer on high speed, whip the cream with the powdered sugar until soft peaks form. Set aside.

FOR ASSEMBLY
1 graham cracker, crushed

TO ASSEMBLE: Dollop the lemon curd on top of each meringue, add a spoonful of whipped cream, and sprinkle graham cracker crumbs on top before serving.

Sugar Cookie Fruit Pizza

If there's anything better than sharing a giant sugar cookie, it's slathering it with orange cream cheese frosting and topping it with fresh fruit. This mini fruit pizza cuts into four little slices.

YIELD · ONE 4-SLICE PIZZA

3 tablespoons unsalted butter, softened

¼ cup granulated sugar

1 large egg yolk

½ teaspoon vanilla extract

½ cup all-purpose flour

⅛ teaspoon baking powder

3 ounces cream cheese, softened

¼ cup powdered sugar

1 to 2 tablespoons fresh orange juice

Fresh fruit, for decorating

Preheat the oven to 350°F and line a baking sheet with parchment paper.

In a small bowl, beat together the butter and sugar with an electric mixer on medium speed. Beat until light and fluffy.

Add the egg yolk and vanilla, and beat until combined.

Sprinkle the flour and baking powder on top of the mixture.

Beat until the dough comes together.

Form the dough into a ball and press it flat into a 6-inch disk on the baking sheet.

Bake for 10 to 12 minutes.

Let the cookie cool completely, leaving it on the baking sheet.

When ready to serve, beat together the cream cheese, powdered sugar, and 1 tablespoon of orange juice with an electric mixer on medium speed until light and fluffy. Add additional orange juice as needed to achieve a spreadable consistency.

Frost the cookie with the cream cheese, decorate with fresh fruit, slice, and serve.

Strawberry Jam Heart Thumbprints

The absolute cutest way to make heart thumbprints is like this: instead of using your thumb, use the side of your pinky to make a cute heart-shaped indent! My Strawberry Jam Heart Thumbprints are not only adorable, they're also delicious. Melt-in-your-mouth shortbread base with a sticky, sweet jelly center. These are perfect as Valentine's Day cookies, but I make them all year!

YIELD · 20 COOKIES

8 tablespoons (1 stick) unsalted butter, softened

¼ cup granulated sugar

1 egg

½ teaspoon vanilla extract

¼ teaspoon almond extract

1 cup all-purpose flour

¼ teaspoon salt

10 teaspoons strawberry jam

Line a large baking sheet with a silicone mat and make room in your fridge for a cookie sheet.

In a large bowl, add the softened butter and beat with an electric mixer on high until light and fluffy. The color of the butter will change from bright yellow to a much paler yellow.

Next, stream in the sugar while beating.

Then, beat in the egg, vanilla, and almond extract and mix very well.

Finally, evenly sprinkle the flour and salt on the dough. Mix the dough with the electric mixer until it just comes together. It might be a bit crumbly, but the heat of your hands will bring it together.

Scoop out 2 teaspoons of dough and use your hands to roll it into a ball, and then place it on a baking sheet.

When all of the cookies are rolled out, dip your pinky in flour and lay it sideways on each dough ball to make half of a heart. Repeat with more flour to make the other half of the heart.

Place ¼ teaspoon of jam on each side of the heart, for a total of ½ teaspoon of jam per heart.

Place the cookies in the fridge for 1 hour to chill before baking. Do not skip this step!

Preheat the oven to 350°F.

Take the baking sheet out of the fridge and bake the cookies for 12 minutes, until the edges are just starting to turn golden brown. Let the cookies cool completely on the baking sheet. Once cool, remove the cookies from the sheet. Shortbread cookies are delicate when warm, so this is why I recommend cooling them on the sheet.

Peanut Butter Bars

The name—peanut butter bars—sounds normal, but the flavor is very unique here. This might be the only time you've seen peanut butter without its other half, chocolate. It's rare for me to keep the two apart. (Please tell me I'm not the only one who dips a spoon in peanut butter and rolls it in mini chocolate chips as an afternoon snack!)

But when it comes to these bars, think of them like a lemon bar . . . but with peanut butter! It's different than anything you've ever had before, but I'm a big fan of widening your dessert horizons.

YIELD · 2 GENEROUS SERVINGS

7 tablespoons unsalted butter, at room temperature

¼ cup powdered sugar, plus extra for serving

¾ cup + 1 tablespoon + ¼ cup all-purpose flour

½ teaspoon fine sea salt, divided

¼ cup peanut butter

½ cup + 2 tablespoons granulated sugar

2 large eggs

Preheat the oven to 350°F and line a loaf pan with parchment paper, leaving excess paper for handles to remove the bars.

In a medium bowl, stir together the butter, powdered sugar, ¾ cup plus 1 tablespoon of the flour, and ¼ teaspoon salt using a spatula.

Press the dough evenly into the bottom of the loaf pan and bake for 20 minutes, until lightly golden brown on the edges. Don't be afraid of a little color.

Meanwhile, wipe out the bowl and use it to beat together the remaining ingredients: peanut butter, remaining ¼ cup flour, granulated sugar, eggs, and remaining ¼ teaspoon salt. Beat with an electric mixer until light and fluffy, about 1 minute.

When the crust is done, pour the peanut butter mixture on top and return it to the oven for 20 to 25 minutes, until the top is dry and starting to crackle.

Cool the bars in the pan for 5 minutes, then remove using the parchment handles.

Slice in half and serve with extra powdered sugar sprinkled on top.

Buttered Grits Cookies
with Lime Glaze

Normally, I'm a spicy grits kind of girl. I love a hot bowl of grits sprinkled with sharp Cheddar cheese and pickled jalapeños. In the summertime, I love a bowl with fresh cherry tomatoes from the garden. So, grits in a dessert? Why not? These cookies have the texture of a muffin top—soft and cakey. You can frequently find me eating these for breakfast, and I won't stop you from doing the same!

YIELD · 12 COOKIES

3 tablespoons stone-ground grits (I use white hominy grits)

½ cup + 1 tablespoon water

¼ teaspoon salt

4 tablespoons (½ stick) unsalted butter, plus butter for pan (optional)

½ cup granulated sugar

1 large egg

½ teaspoon vanilla extract

1 cup all-purpose flour

½ teaspoon baking powder

1 cup powdered sugar

Juice of 1 lime

Place the grits, water, and salt in a 2-cup glass measuring cup and stir. Microwave on high for 90 seconds. Stir the mixture, and then microwave for another 30 seconds. The mixture should not overflow the cup, but if it does, start over, as the amount of liquid in the recipe will then be off.

Pour the grits into a medium mixing bowl, and let cool for 15 minutes.

Preheat the oven to 350°F and line a baking sheet with parchment paper or a silicone mat.

Once the grits have cooled, stir in the butter. It will melt completely. Next, stir in the sugar, egg, and vanilla. Stir until very well combined.

Sprinkle the flour and baking powder on top of the grits mixture. Stir to combine.

Scoop out 12 equal portions of the dough onto the cookie sheet about 1½ inches apart.

Bake for 11 to 13 minutes, or until the surface of the cookies appears dry and the edges are just beginning to brown.

Meanwhile, in a small bowl, mix together the powdered sugar and lime juice. Drizzle over the cookies. Serve warm.

Gingerbread Blondies
with Lemon Glaze

My small-batch blondies made in an 8-inch square pan are practically famous (you can always trust a non-chocolate lover to make incredible blondies), and with the addition of some gingerbread spices (ground ginger, allspice, nutmeg, and cloves), they're even better. I hope you don't mind that these serve slightly more than two people. The recipe makes 15 little three-bite Christmas tree shapes—a great addition to a holiday cookie plate!

YIELD · 15 BLONDIES

FOR THE BLONDIES
8 tablespoons (1 stick) unsalted butter

1½ cups dark brown sugar

1½ teaspoons vanilla extract

½ teaspoon fine sea salt

1 egg + 1 egg yolk

1½ cups all-purpose flour

¾ teaspoon baking powder

¾ teaspoon ground ginger

½ teaspoon ground cinnamon

½ teaspoon ground allspice

½ teaspoon freshly grated nutmeg

¼ teaspoon ground cloves

Preheat the oven to 350°F and line an 8-inch square baking dish with two pieces of parchment paper or foil in both directions (leave excess on one piece of parchment to use as a handle for lifting out of the pan).

In a microwave-safe bowl, melt the butter in 20-second intervals.

Next, stir in the brown sugar, vanilla, and salt.

Stir in the whole eggs and the egg yolk and stir until very well incorporated.

Finally, sprinkle the flour, spices, and baking powder on top and stir until well mixed and no streaks of flour remain.

Pour the blondie batter into the prepared pan and bake it on the center rack of the oven for about 23 minutes, testing every few minutes after the 23-minute mark. Moist crumbs should cling to a toothpick inserted into the center, but you shouldn't see any wet batter on the toothpick.

Let cool in the pan for about 10 minutes, and then lift the blondies out and let them cool completely on a cooling rack.

To slice the blondies into triangles, slice into three long strips, slice off the ends, and then alternate the angle of the knife to cut triangles.

FOR THE LEMON GLAZE

1½ cups powdered sugar

4 teaspoons fresh lemon juice, plus the lemon zest

1 large egg white (pasteurized, if you prefer)

Once the blondies are completely cool, make the glaze by whisking together the powdered sugar, lemon juice, and egg white. Resist the urge to add more liquid to make the glaze come together, just whisk slowly and it will all come together in a few minutes.

Drizzle the icing across the triangles. Before the icing dries, sprinkle the lemon zest on top.

Oatmeal Cream Pies

The thing is, these oatmeal cookies are so good on their own — so chewy, spicy, and warm—that they don't even really need the marshmallow filling. But they're not worse with marshmallow filling, so pile it on!

YIELD • 5 SANDWICH COOKIES

FOR THE COOKIES

½ cup rolled oats

¾ cup all-purpose flour

¾ teaspoon cornstarch

½ teaspoon baking powder

⅛ teaspoon baking soda

⅛ teaspoon salt

½ teaspoon ground cinnamon

⅛ teaspoon freshly grated nutmeg

⅛ teaspoon ground ginger

3 tablespoons unsalted butter, at room temperature

2 tablespoons solid vegetable shortening

3 tablespoons molasses

½ cup granulated sugar

½ teaspoon vanilla extract

1 large egg yolk

FOR THE MARSHMALLOW FILLING

1 cup marshmallow cream

2 tablespoons unsalted butter, at room temperature

2 tablespoons solid vegetable shortening

½ cup powdered sugar

Preheat the oven to 350°F and line a cookie sheet with parchment paper.

TO MAKE THE COOKIES: In a food processor, pulse the oats 10 times, for 1 to 2 seconds, just to break them up a bit. Do not grind them to a flour.

In a small bowl, whisk together the oats, flour, cornstarch, baking powder, baking soda, salt, and spices. Whisk very well.

In a medium bowl, using an electric mixer on medium speed, cream together the butter, shortening, molasses, sugar, and vanilla for at least 45 seconds, scraping the bowl as necessary to incorporate evenly. Finally, beat in the egg yolk. Add the dry ingredients to this mixture in two batches, beating well to combine.

Make 10 golf ball–size dough balls with your hands. Space them equally apart on the prepared cookie sheet, and then press them flat with your hands.

Bake for 10 to 12 minutes, or until fragrant and the tops look dry. Don't overbake, because they will continue to cook a bit while they cool on the pan.

Let cool on the cookie sheet for 5 minutes, then move to a cooling rack.

TO MAKE THE FILLING: Once the cookies have cooled, using an electric mixer on high speed, beat together all the filling ingredients in a medium bowl. Divide it among five of the cookies, and then press another cookie on top of each to form five sandwiches.

Salted Caramel Bars

This recipe is calling your name, I just know it. Buttery rich shortbread sandwiched by salted caramel. It doesn't get much better than this.

   I'm going to give you my recipe for salted caramel sauce, but a jarred version is totally fine here. My recipe makes 1 cup of caramel sauce, and you'll only need ¼ cup, plus a little extra for drizzling, to make these bars. While I'm normally averse to leftover dessert, I make an exception for salted caramel sauce. Put it in a jar in the fridge, and you'll find plenty of things to use it in throughout the week.

YIELD • 2 GENEROUS SERVINGS

FOR THE BARS
7 tablespoons unsalted butter, at room temperature

¼ cup powdered sugar

¾ cup + 1 tablespoon all-purpose flour

⅛ teaspoon fine sea salt

¼ cup Salted Caramel Sauce (recipe follows), or use store-bought, plus extra for drizzling

MAKE THE BARS: Preheat the oven to 350°F.

Line a bread loaf pan with parchment paper, making sure to leave enough excess to make handles to help you move it out of the pan.

In a small bowl, combine the butter, powdered sugar, flour, and salt. Using a pastry blender, two knives, or simply your fingers, blend the butter into the flour mixture until a soft, crumbly dough forms.

Press three-quarters of the dough onto the bottom of the loaf pan and press it flat.

Spread ¼ cup of caramel sauce on top.

Dot the remaining dough over the top of the caramel sauce, focusing on the edges.

Bake for 30 minutes.

Let the bars cool slightly, then lift them out of the pan to cool completely.

Before serving, drizzle extra caramel sauce on top, if desired (it's very desirable).

FOR THE SALTED CARAMEL SAUCE

1 cup granulated sugar

¼ cup water

½ cup + 2 tablespoons half-and-half (or cream)

1 tablespoon unsalted butter

1 teaspoon fine sea salt

1 teaspoon pure vanilla extract

MAKE THE CARAMEL SAUCE, IF USING: In a deep saucepan (at least 2 quarts—no smaller, because the mixture bubbles up!), add the sugar and water. Whisk to combine.

Turn the heat to medium-high and let the sugar melt and dissolve without stirring. If you see sugar crystals on the sides of the pan, use a pastry brush dipped in water to gently push them back in the pan. Do not stir.

Once the sugar is dissolved, crank the heat to high and watch it turn an amber color. Watch closely, it happens quickly! You can swirl the pan gently to evenly brown the caramel.

Meanwhile, heat the half-and-half (or cream) until it's steaming and small bubbles are forming around the edges.

Turn off the heat to the sugar mixture and add the half-and-half all at once. Be careful—it bubbles up triple the size! It is very hot!

Next, whisk in the butter, salt, and vanilla. Whisk until smooth. Pour the mixture into a jar to cool and use as you like.

A Dozen Rummy Oatmeal Cookies

I purposefully did not include the word *raisin* in the recipe title, because I know a lot of people have serious disdain for raisins. I'm not sure why this is; they're just dried grapes. However, I think if you're a raisin hater, you just might be convinced with this recipe because I soak them in rum before stirring them into the cookie batter. If not, substitute chocolate chips.

YIELD · 12 COOKIES

½ cup raisins

2 tablespoons dark rum

3 tablespoons unsalted butter, at room temperature

3 tablespoons light brown sugar

3 tablespoons granulated sugar

1 large egg yolk

¼ cup + 2 tablespoons all-purpose flour

¼ + ⅛ teaspoon baking powder

¼ teaspoon baking soda

¼ + ⅛ teaspoon ground cinnamon

⅛ teaspoon ground allspice

⅛ teaspoon salt

½ cup rolled oats

Preheat the oven to 350°F and have ready a baking sheet.

In a small bowl, stir together the raisins and rum. Set aside and let soak.

In a medium bowl, cream together the butter and sugars for 1 to 2 minutes. Once thoroughly combined, add the egg yolk.

In a small bowl, whisk together the flour, baking powder, baking soda, cinnamon, allspice, and salt. Add half of the flour mixture to the butter mixture, mixing until just combined. Add the remaining flour mixture, and beat until combined. Do not overmix. Stir in the oats and raisins (include any rum that was not absorbed).

Divide equally into 12 balls, and space 1 inch apart on the baking sheet.

Bake for 13 to 15 minutes, or until golden brown. Don't be afraid to let these cookies get a little color—the browned butter and rum flavor combo is delicious.

Mud Hens

Desserts with the strangest names always taste the best, in my book. Mud hens are a type of cookie bar. The bottom layer is cookie dough studded with chocolate chips. The cookie layer is then topped with nuts and marshmallows, and everything is crowned in a beautiful crisp meringue. You want to let these bars cool in the pan for at least an hour, but remove them after that so the crust can firm up.

YIELD • 2 BARS

5 tablespoons unsalted butter, at room temperature

6 tablespoons granulated sugar

1 large egg, separated

½ cup + 1 tablespoon all-purpose flour

⅛ teaspoon baking powder

⅛ teaspoon salt

2 tablespoons semisweet chocolate chips

¼ cup chopped pecans

¼ cup mini marshmallows

2 tablespoons light brown sugar

Preheat the oven to 350°F and line a 9-by-5-inch loaf pan with parchment paper.

In a medium bowl, using an electric mixer on medium speed, beat together the remaining 1 tablespoon of shortening, butter, and granulated sugar. Beat this mixture very well before adding the egg yolk and continuing to beat.

Sprinkle the flour, baking powder, and salt over the top and beat until the dough comes together in a mass. At first it will be crumbly, but keep beating and it will firm up. Spread the dough evenly in the bottom of the prepared loaf pan, using a silicone spatula.

Sprinkle the chocolate chips on top, lightly pressing them into the dough. Then sprinkle the marshmallows and pecans.

Using an electric mixer on high speed, beat the egg white until stiff. Add the brown sugar and fold it in well. Spread it on top of the nuts and marshmallows. Don't worry if the marshmallows and nuts get all mixed up into the meringue—this is good.

Bake for 22 to 24 minutes, until the meringue is nicely browned. Let cool in the pan for an hour before removing them from the pan (or else the bottom might get soggy). Slice in half and serve.

Texas Ranger Cookies

When I visit home, these cookies are always in the cookie jar waiting for me. There's something so addictive about soft, chewy cookies punctuated with crispy cornflakes. The best way to describe these cookies is that they taste like caramel, with crunchy bits.

YIELD • 8 COOKIES

¼ cup solid vegetable shortening

3 tablespoons granulated sugar

¼ cup packed light brown sugar

1 large egg white

¼ teaspoon vanilla extract

¼ teaspoon salt

½ cup all-purpose flour

¼ teaspoon baking powder

3 tablespoons natural (unsweetened) dessicated coconut

2 tablespoons rolled oats

⅓ cup (heaping) cornflakes

Preheat the oven to 350°F and position a rack in the center of the oven.

Line a cookie sheet with a silicone mat or parchment paper.

In a medium bowl, using an electric mixer on medium speed, cream together the shortening, granulated sugar, and brown sugar very well, about 45 seconds. Add the egg white, vanilla, and salt. Beat for 15 seconds to combine well.

Sprinkle the flour and baking powder evenly over the dough. Add all the remaining ingredients on top. Beat the dough together for about 10 seconds to combine and crush the cornflakes.

Scoop eight equal dough balls and space them evenly on the prepared cookie sheet. Bake for 12 minutes.

Let cool for 1 minute on the cookie sheet, and then move to a cooling rack to cool completely.

Forgotten Cookies

With this recipe comes zero guarantees that you will be able to resist a breakfast of cookies. The premise of these cookies is this: Preheat the oven at night, mix up the cookie dough, place it in the oven, turn off the oven, and sleep for 8 hours. In the morning, you'll have crisp meringue cookies. They sound much better than a bowl of cereal, don't they?

YIELD · 6 COOKIES

1 large egg white, at room temperature

⅓ cup granulated sugar

½ teaspoon vanilla extract

½ cup chocolate chips

½ cup chopped nuts (pecans, almonds, anything you like)

½ cup sweetened shredded coconut

Preheat the oven to 350°F. Ensure it reaches this temperature before proceeding.

Line a cookie sheet with foil. Do not skip the foil.

In a medium bowl, beat the egg white until very stiff either by hand, using a large whisk, or using an electric mixer on high speed. Soft peaks will make cookies that spread—make sure you beat the egg white until stiff.

Beat in the sugar and vanilla. Fold in the remaining ingredients.

Scoop six equal portions of the batter onto the prepared cookie sheet, leaving at least 2 inches of space between the cookies.

Place the cookies in the oven, close the door, and then turn off the oven. Let the cookies sit without opening the door for 8 full hours. No peeking!

Store the cookies in an airtight jar so they stay crisp.

Chai Bars

You probably know by now how much of a tea lover I am; there's hardly a way that I haven't crammed tea into my desserts.

These gooey chai bars are my favorite chai-flavored dessert (until I make the next one), but if you lack all of these spices, go ahead and make it just with cinnamon (1½ teaspoons total). You'll still get a warm, gooey spice bar that tastes the best first thing in the morning.

YIELD · 2 GENEROUS SERVINGS

FOR THE BARS

¼ teaspoon ground ginger

½ teaspoon ground cardamom

¼ teaspoon freshly ground black pepper

¼ teaspoon ground cloves

½ teaspoon ground cinnamon

1 cup all-purpose flour

½ teaspoon baking powder

⅛ teaspoon baking soda

5⅓ tablespoons unsalted butter, melted

1 cup brown sugar

1 large egg

¾ teaspoon vanilla extract

FOR THE TOPPING

½ reserved teaspoon of the spice mixture (from above)

⅛ cup granulated sugar

1 tablespoon unsalted butter, melted

Preheat the oven to 350°F and line a loaf pan with parchment paper to prevent sticking.

Combine all of the spices together in a small bowl and set aside.

Next, whisk together the flour, all of the spices except ½ teaspoon (reserve it for topping after baking), baking powder, and baking soda.

In a separate bowl, whisk together the melted butter, brown sugar, eggs, and vanilla.

Stir the wet ingredients into the dry until no streaks of flour remain.

Pour the batter into the prepared pan and bake for 20 minutes.

Start testing the bars at 17 minutes—you want them to bake but still be soft in the center. Wet crumbs clinging to the toothpick are okay, but the top should be dry to the touch.

While the bars are still warm, make the topping: Melt the butter. Stir the granulated sugar and reserved spice mixture into the butter and brush on the bars.

Let cool, slice, and serve.

Big Salty Chocolate Chip Cookies
with Caramel

This recipe makes six giant chocolate chip cookies. That's three for me, three for you. Or, if like me, you want all six, please *eat all the cookies*. And then tell me all about it so I feel better about myself. Thanks!

YIELD · 6 LARGE COOKIES

4 tablespoons (½ stick) unsalted butter, at room temperature

3 tablespoons light brown sugar

2 tablespoons granulated sugar

1 large egg yolk

¾ teaspoon vanilla extract

½ cup all-purpose flour

¼ teaspoon instant espresso powder (optional)

¼ teaspoon baking powder

⅓ cup chocolate chunks

5 caramel candies, cut into 18 pieces

Flaky sea salt, for sprinkling

Preheat the oven to 375°F and line a baking sheet with parchment paper.

In a medium bowl, with an electric mixer on medium speed, beat together the butter and sugars.

Once creamy, add the egg yolk and vanilla and beat to combine.

In a small bowl, whisk together the flour, espresso powder (if using), and baking powder.

Add the dry ingredients to the butter mixture and beat until just combined.

Meanwhile, chop the chocolate chunks into smaller pieces, being careful to save all the fine bits. Add this to the dough and stir to evenly distribute.

Divide the dough into six equal pieces, and make large balls of dough by rolling it between your hands. Space the cookies evenly on a baking sheet.

Press three pieces of caramel candy close to the center of each dough ball. Be careful not to press the dough balls flat. Also, since the cookies will spread quite a bit, it's best to keep the caramel pieces very close together.

Bake for 10 minutes, or until the edges of the cookies start to brown. Sprinkle the cookies generously with salt. Let cool on the baking sheet for 2 minutes before moving to a wire rack to cool completely.

CAKES

&

CUPCAKES

Matcha Layer Cake

A bright green cake with fluffy white buttercream sandwiched between the layers and fresh strawberries on top is so stunning for almost any occasion. This simple matcha cake is made with green tea powder (also known as matcha) and baked in a single 8-inch square pan that you easily slice and stack to make a two-layer loaf cake.

YIELD • ONE 8-INCH CAKE

FOR THE CAKE
7 tablespoons unsalted butter, softened

1 cup granulated sugar

2 large eggs

1½ tablespoons matcha powder

1 teaspoon vanilla extract

1 cup all-purpose flour

1 teaspoon baking powder

⅓ cup buttermilk

TO MAKE THE CAKE: Preheat the oven to 325°F and line the bottom of an 8-inch square pan with parchment paper. Lightly spray the exposed sides of the lined pan with cooking spray.

In a medium bowl, using an electric mixer on medium speed, beat together the softened butter and sugar until light and fluffy, 1 to 2 minutes.

Add the eggs, matcha powder, and vanilla, and beat until just combined.

In a small bowl, whisk together the flour and baking powder.

Add half of the flour mixture to the bowl and stir to combine.

Add all of the buttermilk and stir again.

Finally, add the remaining half of the flour mixture and stir until no streaks of flour remain, but be careful not to overmix the batter.

Scrape the batter into the prepared pan and bake on the middle rack for 30 to 33 minutes, until a toothpick inserted comes out mostly clean with only moist crumbs (not wet batter).

Let the cake cool in the pan for about 15 minutes, until it starts to pull away from the edges of the pan. Then, run a knife around the edge of the cake and lift it out of the pan; place on a cooling rack to cool completely.

FOR THE FROSTING

8 tablespoons (1 stick) unsalted butter, softened

2 cups powdered sugar, sifted

1½ teaspoons vanilla extract

2 tablespoons heavy cream

Fresh strawberries, optional for garnish

TO MAKE THE FROSTING: Combine all frosting ingredients in a bowl. Then, beat all of the frosting ingredients together until light and fluffy.

Slice the cake in half (from one square into two rectangles) and spread some buttercream on top of one half. Place the opposite cake half on top of the cake half with buttercream.

Decorate the cake with the remaining buttercream, powdered sugar, and fresh strawberries. Slice into five or six triangles and serve.

Hummingbird Cupcakes

Hummingbird cake is a very popular Southern recipe that frequently graced the table when I was growing up. It is a soft white cake full of banana, pineapple, coconut, and pecans. These ingredients were considered special during our grandparents' time and were saved for the holiday season. Since ingredients are available all year these days, you can make these cupcakes any time of year. The brown sugar cream cheese frosting on top is the perfect accompaniment to the multitude of flavors in the cupcake below.

YIELD · 4 CUPCAKES

FOR THE CUPCAKES

3 tablespoons canola oil

½ small banana

⅓ cup sugar

¼ cup crushed pineapple, lightly drained

2 tablespoons sweetened coconut shreds

1 large egg

⅛ teaspoon almond extract

⅓ cup + 3 tablespoons all-purpose flour

¼ teaspoon baking powder

¼ teaspoon cinnamon

Pinch of salt

FOR THE FROSTING

3 ounces cream cheese, softened

2 tablespoons unsalted butter, softened

2 tablespoons dark brown sugar

3 to 5 tablespoons powdered sugar

Toasted pecans for garnish

TO MAKE THE CUPCAKES: Preheat the oven to 350°F and line a muffin pan with four cups. Gather all ingredients for the cupcakes and have the frosting ingredients resting on the counter coming to room temperature while you bake.

In a medium bowl, stir together the canola oil, banana, and sugar. Mash the banana into the oil and sugar mixture.

Once it's well incorporated, stir in the pineapple, coconut, egg, and almond extract and mix well. Sprinkle the flour, baking powder, cinnamon, and salt on top. Stir until just combined but don't overmix.

Divide the batter between the four cups and bake for 18 to 21 minutes, or until a toothpick inserted comes out clean. Let cool completely before frosting.

TO MAKE THE FROSTING: Beat together the cream cheese, butter, and brown sugar.

Begin by adding 3 tablespoons of the powdered sugar and beating it together well. If the frosting is too stiff, add the remaining powdered sugar.

Frost the cupcakes and serve.

Peppermint Brownie Bites

I can always seem to find a reason to bake four little brownie bites. No matter the season, these brownie bites are welcome. When peppermint doesn't sound good, sprinkles do. Or mini chocolate chips. Or crushed cookies. You have seriously delicious options with this recipe!

YIELD • 4 MINI BROWNIES

FOR THE BROWNIE BITES

3 tablespoons unsalted butter, plus extra for greasing the pan

7 tablespoons granulated sugar

¼ cup cocoa powder

¼ teaspoon fine sea salt

¼ teaspoon peppermint extract

1 large egg

3 tablespoons all-purpose flour

FOR DUNKING

½ cup chopped chocolate

1 tablespoon coconut oil

10 peppermint candies, crushed

Preheat the oven to 350°F and grease four cups in a muffin pan very well with butter.

Next, combine the butter, sugar, and cocoa powder in a small bowl and microwave at full power for 30 seconds. Stir very well and repeat.

Stir the salt and peppermint extract into the warm batter, then stir for about a minute to cool off the mixture. Then stir in the egg.

Finally, sprinkle the flour over the top and stir into the batter using about 50 strokes. (You want to stir the flour very well to activate the gluten and make a chewy brownie.)

Bake the bites for 15 minutes, then remove from the oven.

Fill a shallow bowl with crushed peppermint candies for dipping.

Meanwhile, add the chopped chocolate and coconut oil to a small bowl. Microwave at 50 percent power for 30 seconds. Stir and repeat. After 1 minute, a few unmelted pieces of chocolate may remain, but that's fine: Let the mixture rest on the counter for 1 minute and stir again. It should all be smooth by now.

Take each warm brownie bite from the pan, dunk in chocolate, and roll in crushed peppermint.

I usually serve these warm, but if you want the chocolate to harden, place them in the fridge for 15 minutes.

Black Forest Cake

If we're being totally honest with each other, my favorite way to eat chocolate is with some fruit. Chocolate and cherries were made for each other. The frosting for this cake is another chance to use up dark cocoa powder if you have it. It tastes great with either regular or dark cocoa, but stick to regular cocoa for the cake part!

YIELD · ONE 6-INCH CAKE

FOR THE CAKE

½ cup all-purpose flour

5 tablespoons cocoa powder

½ teaspoon baking soda

¼ teaspoon fine sea salt

⅓ cup canola oil

½ cup granulated sugar

⅓ cup full-fat sour cream

1 large egg

½ teaspoon vanilla extract

1 tablespoon warm water

FOR THE FROSTING

½ cup heavy cream

¼ cup powdered sugar

2 tablespoons cocoa powder (dark or regular)

FOR GARNISH

20 fresh dark sweet cherries, pitted

Powdered sugar

TO MAKE THE CAKE: Preheat the oven to 350°F and line the bottom of a 6-inch round cake pan with a circle of parchment paper. Then spray the pan with cooking spray.

In a small bowl, whisk together the flour, cocoa, baking soda, and salt.

In a medium bowl, stir together the oil and sugar with a wooden spoon. Add the sour cream and stir until well blended. Next, add the egg and vanilla. Stir until combined.

Sprinkle half of the flour mixture on the wet mixture. Stir until well blended. Then stir in the water, followed by the remaining flour. Stir until no streaks of flour remain.

Scrape the batter into the cake pan and bake on a baking sheet for 30 minutes. Test with a toothpick to ensure it's done (an underdone cake will sink as it cools).

TO MAKE THE FROSTING: While the cake is cooling, beat together all of the frosting ingredients with an electric mixer until light and fluffy, like whipped cream. This will take 2 to 3 minutes.

Once the cake is cool, run a knife around the edge and gently tip it out of the pan. Turn it upside down and frost. Refrigerate until ready to serve.

TO GARNISH: Top with cherries, sprinkle with powdered sugar, and serve.

Chocolate Ganache Cupcakes
with Peppermint Crunch (or Sprinkles!)

A small batch of chocolate cupcakes with simple, perfect chocolate ganache. For the holidays, I love to top them with crushed candy canes. But every other month of the year, sprinkles work quite nicely.

YIELD · 10 ONE-BITE CUPCAKES

FOR THE CUPCAKES

⅓ cup all-purpose flour

2 tablespoons unsweetened cocoa powder

¼ teaspoon baking soda

¼ teaspoon baking powder

¼ teaspoon instant espresso powder (optional)

4 teaspoons canola oil

½ teaspoon vanilla extract

¼ cup lightly packed light brown sugar

⅓ cup low-fat buttermilk

FOR THE CHOCOLATE GANACHE

¼ cup dark chocolate chips

2 tablespoons unsalted butter

⅛ teaspoon peppermint extract (or vanilla, if you're topping the cupcakes with sprinkles)

2 crushed candy canes (or sprinkles or nuts)

TO MAKE THE CUPCAKES: Preheat the oven to 350°F and line 10 cups of a mini muffin pan with mini cupcake liners.

In a medium bowl, whisk together the flour, cocoa powder, baking soda, baking powder, and espresso powder, if using. Whisk well.

In a separate small bowl, whisk together the canola oil, vanilla, brown sugar, and buttermilk until well combined.

Pour the wet ingredients into the dry ingredients, and stir to combine. Do not overmix. Divide the batter between the 10 prepared cups.

Bake the cupcakes for 8 to 11 minutes. Test a cupcake with a toothpick before removing from the oven. If moist crumbs cling to it, they're baked thoroughly.

Let the cupcakes cool in the pan for 1 minute, then transfer them to a wire rack to cool completely.

TO MAKE THE FROSTING: In a small bowl, melt the chocolate chips and butter in the microwave in 15-second intervals, stirring between each. It should only take 2 to 3 pulses. Stir in the peppermint or vanilla extract once the mixture is melted smooth.

Have the crushed candy canes or sprinkles ready in a shallow bowl. Dip the top of each cupcake in the melted chocolate, and then roll in the crushed candy canes or sprinkles.

You can let the chocolate harden in the fridge for 30 minutes, but do not store the cupcakes in the fridge any longer than that because the candy canes will soften.

Very Vanilla Cupcakes

If there's an occasion in life not improved by four delicious little vanilla cupcakes, I haven't found it. Two each, one for each hand.

FOR THE CUPCAKES

4 tablespoons (½ stick) unsalted butter, at room temperature

¼ cup granulated sugar

1 large egg white

½ teaspoon vanilla extract

2 tablespoons sour cream

6 tablespoons all-purpose flour

½ teaspoon baking soda

Pinch of salt

FOR THE FROSTING

3 ounces cream cheese, softened

2 tablespoons unsalted butter, at room temperature

6 tablespoons powdered sugar

¼ teaspoon vanilla extract

1 tablespoon sour cream

TO MAKE THE CUPCAKES: Preheat the oven to 350°F. Place cupcake liners in four cups along the edge of a muffin pan.

In a medium bowl, using an electric mixer on medium speed, beat together the butter and sugar until fluffy, at least 30 seconds. Next, add the egg white, vanilla, and sour cream. Beat until combined.

Add the flour, baking soda, and salt, and beat until incorporated. Scrape down the sides and bottom of the bowl to ensure the batter is well mixed.

Divide the batter among the prepared muffin cups. Bake for 16 to 18 minutes, or until a toothpick inserted into the center of a cupcake comes out with only moist crumb clinging to it. The cupcakes will spring back when gently pressed, also.

Let cool completely before frosting.

TO MAKE THE FROSTING: In a medium bowl, using an electric mixer on high speed, beat together all of the frosting ingredients. Frost the cupcakes and serve.

Cookies and Cream Cupcakes

Sometimes, the best way to show your love is with a small batch of chocolate cupcakes with cookies-and-cream buttercream frosting on top.

Since I bake for a living, I don't typically allow my husband to have store-bought cookies in the house. It only seems fair that, if I always have freshly baked cookies on the counter, he probably shouldn't go to the store and buy cookies, right? Please take my side. I finally gave in and stopped denying my husband's love for chocolate sandwich cookies. I bought him a box (of organic, all-natural ones, ha!), and he was shocked. Then, when I made Cookies and Cream Cupcakes with them, he was even more shocked!

YIELD · 4 CUPCAKES

FOR THE CUPCAKES
⅓ cup all-purpose flour

2 tablespoons (slightly heaped) unsweetened cocoa powder

¼ teaspoon baking soda

¼ teaspoon baking powder

½ teaspoon instant espresso powder (optional)

⅓ cup buttermilk

4 teaspoons canola oil

½ teaspoon vanilla extract

¼ cup packed dark brown sugar

FOR THE FROSTING
4 tablespoons (½ stick) unsalted butter, softened

1 cup powdered sugar

1 tablespoon heavy cream

½ teaspoon vanilla extract

4 chocolate sandwich cookies

TO MAKE THE CUPCAKES: Preheat the oven to 350°F and line four cups in a muffin pan with paper liners.

In a medium bowl, whisk together the flour, cocoa, baking soda, baking powder, and espresso powder (if using).

Next, in a small measuring cup, thoroughly whisk together the buttermilk, oil, vanilla, and brown sugar.

Add the wet ingredients to the dry ingredients and stir until they're just mixed.

Divide the batter between the cupcake liners and bake for 16 to 17 minutes. They're done when the tops spring back when touched (if you underbake, they'll sink). Let the cupcakes cool completely.

TO MAKE THE FROSTING: In a small bowl, beat together the butter, powdered sugar, heavy cream, and vanilla using an electric mixer on high. Beat the mixture for 1 minute, until it's very fluffy and light.

Finally, stir in the cookies by hand, crushing them as you add them. Frost the cooled cupcakes and serve.

Lemon Cupcakes

Lemon cupcakes made with sour cream and a tangy lemon cream cheese frosting—these are the *best* lemon cupcakes, ever! A cupcake for true lemon lovers only. This small-batch recipe makes four cupcakes but can be scaled up to serve more.

YIELD • 4 CUPCAKES

FOR THE CUPCAKES

4 tablespoons (½ stick) unsalted butter, at room temperature

4 tablespoons granulated sugar

1 egg white

Zest of 1 lemon

¼ teaspoon almond extract

2 tablespoons sour cream

6 tablespoons all-purpose flour

½ teaspoon baking soda

Pinch of salt

FOR THE FROSTING

3 ounces cream cheese, softened

2 tablespoons unsalted butter, softened

6 tablespoons powdered sugar

Juice of ½ lemon

TO MAKE THE CUPCAKES: Preheat the oven to 400°F and place four cupcake liners in a muffin pan. Ensure an oven rack is in the middle position in the oven.

First, place the softened butter in a mixing bowl and add the granulated sugar.

Beat together until fluffy, 1 to 2 minutes.

Next, add the egg white, almond extract, lemon zest, and sour cream.

Beat together all wet ingredients before adding any dry ingredients.

Finally, sprinkle the flour, baking soda, and salt on top. Beat just to combine.

Divide the batter between four cupcake liners in a muffin pan. Bake the cupcakes for 15 to 17 minutes, testing with a toothpick that should come out with only moist crumbs, not wet batter. Let the cupcakes cool completely before attempting to frost, or else the lemon cream cheese frosting might melt!

TO MAKE THE FROSTING: Gather the ingredients for the lemon cream cheese frosting. In a small bowl, with an electric beater on medium-high speed, beat together all the frosting ingredients.

When the mixture is super creamy, you're ready to frost the cupcakes. You can use a butter knife or scrape the frosting into a piping bag to make pretty swirls; it's totally your choice.

Angel Food Cake in a Loaf Pan

Angel food cake is one of my favorite cakes of all time. It's light, airy, and just faintly sweet. The sugar crust on the top is my absolute favorite, and when it's baked in a loaf pan you get plenty of it.

   While this recipe serves slightly more than two people, since you'll get seven or eight slices, it's significantly less than a standard angel food cake recipe. You only need seven egg whites for this recipe.

YIELD · 3 TO 4 SERVINGS

¾ cup granulated sugar, divided

½ cup all-purpose flour

1 tablespoon cornstarch

7 large egg whites

2 teaspoons vanilla extract

¾ teaspoon cream of tartar

¼ teaspoon fine sea salt

Whipped cream, for garnish

Fresh raspberries, for garnish

Preheat the oven to 325°F and have a 9-by-5-inch loaf pan ready. Ensure it is not nonstick. Do not line or grease the pan in any way. Trust me!

In a small bowl, whisk together ¼ cup of the sugar, the flour, and the cornstarch. Set aside.

Add the egg whites, vanilla, cream of tartar, and salt to the bowl of a mini stand mixer. Beat the mixture on medium until it's foamy, about 30 seconds. Slowly stream in the remaining ½ cup of sugar, 1 tablespoon at a time, while the mixer runs. Continue to beat on high speed until soft, floppy peaks form, about 4 minutes.

Next, add one-third of the dry ingredients and gently fold them into the egg whites using a rubber spatula. Proper folding technique is down the middle and around the sides. Your goal is to incorporate the flour mixture without deflating the air you just whipped into the egg whites.

Repeat with the remaining flour mixture in two increments. Take your time; it will take at least 5 minutes to fold everything together gently. Be sure no lumps of flour remain (or they will rise to the surface of your cake while baking).

Pour the batter into the loaf pan. Place the loaf pan on a baking sheet and bake for 38 to 42 minutes. The cake is done when the top is no longer sticky to the touch, and if it cracks, the cracks won't be sticky either.

Once the cake comes out of the oven, immediately turn it upside down and invert it over two cans. The cake needs to cool upside down so it doesn't deflate. Let it cool for at least 60 minutes.

Once the cake is cool, run a knife around the edges of the pan and gently let the cake fall onto a cutting board on its side.

Use a serrated knife to slice the cake into even slices. Go slow and don't smush the cake while slicing.

Serve with whipped cream and raspberries.

Snowball Cake

While the bright pink color of this snowball cake catches your eye, it's the sticky marshmallow frosting that will have you coming back for more. A snowball cake is a chocolate cake with marshmallow frosting and pink-dyed coconut on top. This one is made in a 6-inch cake pan, and we will slice it in half to make a small layer cake.

YIELD · ONE 6-INCH CAKE

FOR THE CAKE

½ cup all-purpose flour

5 tablespoons unsweetened cocoa powder

½ teaspoon baking soda

⅓ cup canola oil

½ cup granulated sugar

⅓ cup full-fat sour cream

1 large egg

½ teaspoon vanilla extract

1 tablespoon warm water or brewed coffee

TO MAKE THE CAKE: Preheat the oven to 350°F and position a rack in the lower third of the oven. Line the bottom of a 6-inch round cake pan with parchment paper and lightly spray with cooking spray.

In a small bowl, whisk together the flour, cocoa powder, and baking soda. Set aside.

In a medium bowl, stir the oil and sugar together, using a wooden spoon. Add the sour cream, and stir until well blended. Next, add the egg and vanilla. Stir until combined.

Sprinkle half of the flour mixture on the sugar mixture. Stir until blended. Stir in the warm water or coffee, followed by the remaining flour mixture. Blend until no streaks of flour remain.

Scrape the batter into the prepared pan, and bake on a cookie sheet for 30 minutes, or until a toothpick inserted into the center comes out with only moist crumbs—if you underbake, the cake will sink as it cools. Be sure to test the toothpick through the entire cake.

Let cool in the pan for 15 minutes, then run a knife around the edge of the pan. The cake should have shrunk away from the edges of the pan, and it should be very easy to remove. Tilt the cake pan on top of a cooling rack, and gently let the cake fall out. Let cool completely before frosting.

FOR THE FLUFFY MARSHMALLOW FROSTING

1 large egg white, cold

½ cup powdered sugar

Pinch of salt

⅛ teaspoon cream of tartar

2 tablespoons boiling water

¼ teaspoon vanilla extract

1½ to 2 cups sweetened shredded coconut

3 to 5 drops red food coloring

TO MAKE THE FROSTING: In a medium bowl, using an electric mixer on low speed, beat together the egg white, powdered sugar, salt, and cream of tartar for 1 minute. Meanwhile, heat the water to a boil. (I usually heat a full cup of water and then scoop out what I need for this recipe—small amounts of water tend to explode in the microwave!)

While beating on low speed, slowly stream in the boiling water. Continue to beat for a full 5 minutes on low speed. The mixture will be thick and glossy, like marshmallow cream. Finally, beat in the vanilla.

Slice the cake in half and spread some marshmallow frosting on top of one half. Place the other half on top of the frosting, and frost entire cake. Stir the coconut and red food coloring together. Decorate the cake with it and serve.

Mini Vanilla Cake

You're going to need a mini 6-inch cake pan with 2-inch sides to make this recipe, but I can nearly promise you that it will be worth it after one bite. Knowing how to make a mini cake is perfect for small celebrations at home. Add sprinkles and it can be a personal birthday cake.

The options are endless, and the buttercream roses are entirely optional!

YIELD • ONE 6-INCH CAKE

FOR THE CAKE
6 tablespoons (¾ stick) unsalted butter, softened

½ cup granulated sugar

1 large egg

1 tablespoon vanilla extract

¾ cup all-purpose flour

⅛ teaspoon fine sea salt

¼ teaspoon baking soda

6 tablespoons buttermilk (see Note)

FOR THE VANILLA BUTTERCREAM
8 tablespoons (1 stick) unsalted butter, at room temperature

2 cups powdered sugar

2 teaspoons vanilla extract

1 tablespoon heavy cream

TO MAKE THE CAKE: Preheat the oven to 350°F and spray a 6-inch round cake pan with cooking spray. Line the bottom of the pan with a round of parchment paper.

In a medium bowl, beat together the butter and sugar with an electric mixer. Beat very well, 1 to 2 minutes.

Add the egg and vanilla, and beat until well combined, about 15 seconds.

In a small bowl, whisk together the flour, salt, and baking soda. Add half of this mixture to the batter and beat for just a few seconds before adding half of the buttermilk. Continue beating the batter. Add the remaining dry ingredients and beat, then add the remaining buttermilk.

Scrape the batter into the prepared pan, smooth out the top, and bake on a small sheet pan for 37 to 39 minutes, until a cake tester comes out clean.

Let the cake cool on a wire rack in the pan. Then run a knife around the edge of the pan and gently tilt the cake out of the pan. Pull away the parchment paper. At this point, you can tightly wrap it in plastic wrap and freeze it for up to 2 months. Let it defrost overnight in the fridge before letting it come to room temperature on the counter. Frost the cake after it has fully defrosted.

TO MAKE THE VANILLA BUTTERCREAM: Beat the butter in a medium bowl with an electric mixer until it's light and fluffy. Add the powdered sugar, vanilla, and heavy cream, and beat until it's light and fluffy again. If the mixture seems too stiff, add a splash more of heavy cream.

NOTE: If you don't have butter-milk on hand or don't want to buy a whole container for just 6 tablespoons, you can make it by combining 6 tablespoons of whole milk with ½ teaspoon of apple cider vinegar. Whisk together and let rest for 5 minutes before using.

Use a little more than half of the buttercream to frost the cake. If you made the cake ahead of time and froze it, it's best to apply a crumb coat of buttercream before applying a thick layer.

Place the remaining quarter of the buttercream in a piping bag fitted with a 1M tip and pipe roses along the outside edge of the cake. To make a rose, pipe a spiral shape: Starting at a center point, pipe the frosting around the center point, moving outward. This is entirely optional but so easy and pretty!

Texas White Sheet Cake

Yes, this cake serves slightly more than two people, but it's still smaller than the average sheet cake, which serves, well, an army. I'm so happy to put our mini baking sheet to use to make a cake that serves four to six people.

I've been loyal to Texas chocolate sheet cake for years, but I've always heard great things about the white/almond version. It doesn't disappoint!

YIELD • 4 TO 6 SERVINGS

FOR THE CAKE

1 cup all-purpose flour

1 cup granulated sugar

⅛ teaspoon fine sea salt

8 tablespoons (1 stick) unsalted butter, melted

¾ cup buttermilk

1 large egg, beaten

½ teaspoon baking soda

½ teaspoon vanilla extract

½ teaspoon almond extract

FOR THE FROSTING

7 tablespoons unsalted butter

3 tablespoons milk

½ teaspoon vanilla extract

¼ teaspoon almond extract

2 heaping cups powdered sugar

½ cup sliced almonds, toasted

TO MAKE THE CAKE: Preheat the oven to 350°F and lightly spray a quarter sheet pan with cooking spray.

First, make the cake: in a medium bowl, whisk together the flour, sugar, and salt.

In a measuring cup, stir together the melted butter, buttermilk, egg, baking soda, vanilla, and almond extract.

Add the buttermilk mixture to the flour mixture.

Stir together all cake ingredients very well, and then pour into the prepared pan.

Bake cake for 15 to 18 minutes, or until an inserted toothpick comes out clean.

TO MAKE THE FROSTING: In a saucepan, melt the butter over medium-low heat.

Stir in the buttermilk and vanilla until well combined.

Remove the pan from the heat and whisk in the powdered sugar.

When the cake comes out of the oven, immediately pour the frosting over it. Use an offset spatula to spread the frosting to the edges of the pan.

Sprinkle with the sliced almonds.

Let the cake cool for at least 30 minutes before serving.

Molten Chocolate Cakes

I've found that ramekins with slightly flared sides work best for this recipe. I use clear glass 6-ounce ramekins with flared edges, instead of straight-sided ramekins.

YIELD · 2 INDIVIDUAL CAKES

⅓ cup semisweet chocolate chips

4 tablespoons (½ stick) unsalted butter

3 tablespoons granulated sugar

½ teaspoon instant espresso powder

¼ teaspoon vanilla extract

1 large egg + 1 large egg yolk

2 tablespoons all-purpose flour

Preheat the oven to 425°F. Spray the ramekins liberally with cooking spray.

In a small bowl, combine the chocolate chips and butter. Microwave on high in 30-second pulses, stirring between each pulse, to melt the chocolate completely.

Once the chocolate has melted, stir in the sugar, espresso powder, and vanilla. Stir for 1 minute to cool the mixture, and then stir in the egg and egg yolk. Stir until combined, and then stir in the flour.

Divide the batter between the prepared ramekins. Bake on a baking sheet for 13 to 14 minutes. The top of the cake should appear well done, but the inside will be runny.

Remove the ramekins from the baking sheet and let cool for 3 minutes before attempting to unmold. If you let the cakes cool completely in the ramekins, the cake will finish cooking all the way.

To unmold, put a small dessert plate on top of the ramekin, flip over, and let the cake fall out gently. Serve immediately.

Mini Chocolate Cake

I like to frost this cake with ganache while it's still in the pan, and then refrigerate it until it's firm. If you're looking for a chocolate buttercream recipe, though, use the recipe from the Mini Vanilla Cake (page 108) and add ⅓ cup of unsweetened Dutch-processed cocoa powder and an extra splash of cream.

YIELD • ONE 6-INCH CAKE

FOR THE CAKE

½ cup all-purpose flour

5 tablespoons unsweetened cocoa powder

½ teaspoon baking soda

⅓ cup neutral oil

½ cup granulated sugar

⅓ cup full-fat sour cream

1 large egg

½ teaspoon vanilla extract

1 tablespoon warm coffee

FOR THE GANACHE

3 ounces semisweet chocolate, chopped

¼ cup heavy cream

Splash of light corn syrup (optional, to keep the frosting super smooth)

FOR THE CAKE: Preheat the oven to 350°F and spray a 6-inch round cake pan with cooking spray. Line the bottom of the pan with a round of parchment paper.

In a medium bowl, whisk together the flour, cocoa powder, and baking soda. Set aside.

In a small bowl, whisk together the oil, sugar, sour cream, egg, vanilla, and coffee.

Add the liquid ingredients to the bowl of dry ingredients, and stir well to combine.

Pour the batter into the cake pan and bake for 29 to 32 minutes, or until a toothpick inserted into the cake comes out clean. It will also start to pull away from the sides when it's done. If you underbake the cake, it will sink slightly.

Let the cake cool on a wire rack in the pan. Then run a knife around the edge of the pan and gently tilt the cake out of the pan. Pull away the parchment paper.

TO MAKE THE GANACHE: In a double boiler or a metal bowl fitted over a pan of simmering water, combine the chopped chocolate, cream, and corn syrup (if using). Stir it over medium heat until it's melted and smooth. Alternatively, you can melt the chocolate and cream in the microwave in 25-second pulses on low power. Stir between each pulse.

Pour the chocolate over the cake and refrigerate it until it's set, about 20 minutes. Serve at room temperature.

Chocolate Orange Cheesecake

If you need a holiday dessert that serves six people or fewer, use this no-bake recipe! After crushing Oreos and pressing them into a loaf pan, make this chocolate orange cheesecake filling to spread on top. You can make this a day ahead of time, and just leave it in the fridge until you're ready to serve.

YIELD • 6 SERVINGS

FOR THE CRUST
15 Oreos (to make 1 cup of crumbs)

3 tablespoons unsalted butter, melted

FOR THE CHEESECAKE FILLING
6 ounces semisweet chocolate, chopped

¾ cup heavy whipping cream

12 ounces (1½ bricks) of full-fat cream cheese, softened to room temperature

¼ cup powdered sugar

1 teaspoon vanilla extract

½ large navel orange, zested (about 1 teaspoon of fresh orange zest)

TO MAKE THE CRUST: Line an 8-inch or 9-inch loaf pan with parchment paper, with enough excess to overhang the edges to form handles to lift out the cheesecake. Give the parchment paper and pan a light spray with cooking spray.

In a food processor or plastic bag, crush the Oreos (keep the cream filling in the cookies). Pour the crumbs into a bowl and stir in the melted butter. Add the crumbs to the loaf pan, and press them into a flat, firm crust.

TO MAKE THE CHEESECAKE FILLING: Place the chopped chocolate in a double boiler to melt (or you can use the microwave on 50% setting and 30-second intervals to melt the chocolate until it's smooth).

Then, in a medium bowl with an electric mixer, beat the heavy cream until medium peaks form.

Scoop the freshly whipped cream out and reserve it in a separate bowl.

Next, add the cream cheese, powdered sugar, vanilla, and orange zest to the bowl that you scraped out the whipped cream from. Beat using an electric mixer until creamy and smooth, about 1 minute.

Using a spatula, fold the melted chocolate into the cream cheese mixture.

Finally, fold the whipped cream gently into the cream cheese mixture. Fold gently to incorporate so that you don't deflate the air bubbles in the whipped cream.

**FOR THE CHOCOLATE
GANACHE TOPPING**
**3 ounces semisweet
chocolate, chopped**

3 tablespoons heavy cream

½ teaspoon orange zest

Scrape the mixture into the loaf pan and make it as flat as possible on top.

Place the pan in the fridge for at least 4 hours or overnight.

If you want the chocolate topping soft, make it just before serving. If you want it to set up like ganache, make it a few hours before and place it back in the fridge.

TO MAKE THE TOPPING: Combine the chopped chocolate and heavy cream in a small bowl. Use a double boiler to melt (or a microwave at 50% power). Once melted and smooth, add the zest from the orange. Pour the chocolate on top of the cheesecake, spreading it to the edges with a spatula. Let it set in the fridge to harden or serve immediately.

Banana Split Cheesecakes

It's a really good thing this recipe makes two individual cheesecakes and not one to share, because I can never share cheesecake!

YIELD · TWO 4½-INCH
CHEESECAKES

4 graham cracker sheets

2 tablespoons unsalted butter, melted

½ cup + 2 teaspoons granulated sugar, divided

8 ounces cream cheese, softened

1 small banana, mashed (2 ounces total)

1 large egg

2 large strawberries (2 ounces total), hulled and diced

2 tablespoons chocolate sauce, plus more for serving

Whipped cream, for serving

Extra strawberries, for serving

Preheat the oven to 350°F. Have ready two 4½-inch mini cheesecake springform pans with removable bottoms.

In a food processor or large plastic bag, crush the graham crackers. Add the melted butter and 2 teaspoons of the sugar and stir to combine.

Divide the crumbs between the prepared pans, pressing them firmly on the bottom and sides of the pans.

Bake the crusts for 7 minutes. After baking, remove the crusts, crack open the oven door, and lower the temperature to 300°F.

In a large bowl, using an electric mixer on medium speed, beat together the remaining ½ cup of sugar with the cream cheese, banana, and egg. Beat very well until homogenous. Pour one-fourth of this mixture into each awaiting crust. Divide the strawberries and sprinkle evenly on top of the cheese mixture. Next, drizzle on the chocolate sauce evenly. Swirl it in with a knife, if desired. Finally, add the remaining cheesecake batter to the pans, and place them on a small baking sheet.

Bake for 30 minutes, or until set in the middle. Let cool completely in the pans and chill overnight for best flavor. To serve, top with whipped cream, extra chocolate sauce, and strawberries.

Warm Carrot Cakes
with Cream Cheese Sauce

If you find yourself in Kansas City, please tell me that you will seek out a barbecue place. It's hard to go wrong with any place—I don't think I've ever had bad barbecue in Kansas City. While the plates of ribs, pulled pork, and brisket blur together in my mind, one thing that stands out is a little place that served warm carrot cake like this one for dessert.

The carrot cakes are baked in small ramekins, tipped out onto a plate before serving while still hot, and drizzled with a warm, melty cream cheese sauce. You will love this!

YIELD · 2 INDIVIDUAL CAKES

FOR THE CAKE
2 tablespoons canola oil

5 tablespoons granulated sugar

1 large egg

½ teaspoon vanilla extract

¼ cup freshly grated carrot

6 tablespoons all-purpose flour

½ teaspoon ground cinnamon

¼ teaspoon ground ginger

⅛ teaspoon freshly grated nutmeg

⅛ teaspoon salt

FOR THE SAUCE
3 ounces cream cheese

1 tablespoon unsalted butter

5 tablespoons powdered sugar

¼ teaspoon vanilla extract

Pecans, for serving (optional)

Preheat the oven to 350°F and spray two 6-ounce ramekins very well with cooking spray. Place the ramekins on a small baking sheet.

TO MAKE THE CAKE: In a medium bowl, whisk together the oil, sugar, egg, vanilla, and grated carrot.

Whisk together the flour, cinnamon, ginger, nutmeg, and salt in a small bowl, and add to the wet ingredients. Stir until well combined.

Divide the mixture equally between the two prepared ramekins; the batter should come almost up to the inner line. Bake on the baking sheet for 23 to 25 minutes, until nicely domed and a toothpick inserted comes out with only moist crumbs.

TO MAKE THE SAUCE: In a small bowl, combine all the sauce ingredients, except the vanilla, and microwave on high in 30-second pulses until melted. Whisk together, and stir in the vanilla. Pour over the cakes and serve.

Pumpkin Donut Holes

Pumpkin donut holes that are coated in irresistible cinnamon-sugar crust: these baked pumpkin spice donut holes taste just like the fried version! It's not just the cinnamon-sugar coating (which all donuts should have, am I right?), there's also a creaminess to the muffins that make them unbelievable, until you try it!

FOR THE DONUT HOLES
4 tablespoons (½ stick) unsalted butter, softened

⅓ cup granulated sugar

1 large egg white

¼ cup canned pumpkin puree

1 cup all-purpose flour

1 teaspoon baking powder

¼ teaspoon salt

¼ cup milk

FOR THE COATING
4 tablespoons (½ stick) unsalted butter, melted

2 tablespoons cinnamon

⅓ cup granulated sugar

Preheat the oven to 350°F and spray nine cups in a mini muffin pan with cooking spray.

TO MAKE THE DONUT HOLES: In a medium bowl, beat together the softened butter and sugar until fluffy, 2 to 3 minutes.

Beat in the egg white and pumpkin puree.

In a small bowl, whisk together the flour, baking powder, and salt.

Add one-third of the dry ingredients to the wet, mixing just to combine.

Add half of the milk; mix well.

Add another third of the dry ingredients, stirring to combine, followed by the last half of the milk.

Finally, stir in the last of the dry ingredients.

Divide the mixture between nine of the mini muffin cups. Do not make more than nine muffins—divide the dough into the pan evenly.

Bake for 12 to 13 minutes, until a toothpick inserted comes out clean.

Let the muffins cool in the pan while making the coating: melt the butter and place in a small bowl for dipping.

Stir the cinnamon and sugar together in a shallow bowl for dipping.

Dip each muffin generously in butter, and then roll in the cinnamon-sugar mixture.

Serve immediately, but they will keep for 1 day covered on the counter.

Banana Bread Bites
with Chai Whip

If banana bread can be improved upon, it is with a dollop of chai whipped cream. Any extra whipped cream is great in a latte, too.

You can also skip the whip and just make 10 mini banana bread muffins using 1 small overripe banana.

FOR THE BANANA BREAD BITES
1 small overripe banana
(6 to 7 inches long)

3 tablespoons unsalted butter, melted

3 tablespoons granulated sugar

2 tablespoons honey

1 large egg yolk

½ cup all-purpose flour

¼ teaspoon baking soda

Pinch of salt

FOR THE CHAI WHIP
⅓ cup heavy whipping cream

¼ teaspoon ground cinnamon

⅛ teaspoon ground cardamom

⅛ teaspoon ground ginger

Pinch of ground cloves

2 tablespoons powdered sugar

TO MAKE THE BANANA BREAD BITES: Preheat the oven to 350°F and spray 10 mini muffin cups with cooking spray.

In a medium bowl, mash the banana very well with a fork. Stir in the melted butter, sugar, honey, and egg yolk. Stir very well.

Sprinkle the flour, baking soda, and salt over the wet ingredients, and then stir to combine.

Divide the batter among the prepared muffin cups, and bake for 13 to 15 minutes. Test the muffins for doneness with a toothpick.

Let the muffins cool for a few minutes in the pan while you make the whipped cream.

TO MAKE THE CHAI WHIP: Beat together the cream with the spices and powdered sugar. Taste, and adjust the sweetness to your taste. You can make the whip a few hours in advance and store in the fridge, which sometimes I prefer because the spices dissolve better in the cream.

Remove the muffins from the pan, and top each with chai whip.

Rise and Shine Blueberry Muffins

Probably our favorite morning treat. I'm constantly finding muffin wrappers in my car because we usually eat them on our hurried way. Delicious muffins I can do, but being punctual, well, I'm still working on that one.

YIELD · 6 MUFFINS

FOR THE MUFFINS
4 tablespoons (½ stick) unsalted butter, melted

½ cup granulated sugar

1 large egg

¾ cup sour cream

1 tablespoon milk

½ teaspoon vanilla extract

½ teaspoon freshly grated lemon zest

1 cup all-purpose flour

1½ teaspoons baking powder

¼ teaspoon baking soda

½ cup fresh or frozen blueberries (if frozen, do not thaw)

FOR THE STREUSEL
2 tablespoons granulated sugar

1 tablespoon all-purpose flour

1 tablespoon cold unsalted butter

Preheat the oven to 400°F and line six cups of a muffin pan with paper liners.

TO MAKE THE MUFFINS: In a medium bowl, stir together the melted butter, sugar, egg, sour cream, milk, vanilla, and lemon zest.

In a small bowl, whisk together the flour, baking powder, and baking soda. Add this to the wet ingredients, and stir gently to combine. Finally, stir in the blueberries.

Fill each prepared muffin cup with the batter—it will come almost to the top.

TO MAKE THE STREUSEL: In the same bowl in which you mixed the dry ingredients, mix all the streusel ingredients together. Use your fingertips to work the butter into the flour and sugar. Sprinkle this mixture evenly over the six muffins.

Bake the muffins on the middle rack of the oven for 16 to 18 minutes, using a toothpick to test for doneness. Let the muffins cool for 1 minute in the pan, and then transfer to a wire rack to cool completely.

Upside-Down Banana Cake

As pretty as it is delicious!

YIELD · ONE 6-INCH CAKE

1 small banana, sliced into ½-inch coins

5 tablespoons unsalted butter, divided, plus extra for greasing the pan

3 tablespoons brown sugar

8 teaspoons granulated sugar

1 large egg

½ teaspoon vanilla extract

¼ teaspoon almond extract

½ cup all-purpose flour

⅛ teaspoon fine sea salt

¾ teaspoon baking powder

⅓ cup milk

Preheat the oven to 350°F and line the bottom of a 6-inch round cake pan with a circle of parchment paper.

Butter the sides of the pan, too.

Place the banana slices in concentric circles in the bottom of the pan.

In a small bowl, combine 2 tablespoons of the butter and the brown sugar. Microwave at full power until melted and bubbling, about 40 seconds. Pour this mixture evenly over the bananas in the pan.

Next, using an electric mixer on medium speed, beat together the remaining 3 tablespoons of butter with the granulated sugar, about 30 seconds.

Add the egg, vanilla, and almond extract and beat until combined.

Sprinkle the flour, salt, and baking powder evenly over the batter. Beat to combine.

Finally, quickly beat in the milk.

Pour the batter over the bananas in the pan.

Bake for 30 minutes, or until the cake is starting to turn golden brown on the top and a toothpick inserted about halfway comes out clean. The cake will also start to pull away from the edges of the pan and you'll hear the bananas simmering.

Let the cake cool for 10 minutes, invert onto a serving plate, and serve.

Mini Jelly Roll

I'm not sure why the simple jelly roll cake has fallen out of favor. It was my grandmother's favorite cake, and very common in her day. I think it's because the cake comes together with simple pantry items. Just open a jar of your favorite jam, roll it up in the cake, slice, and serve. Don't be scared of rolling the cake. The batter is spongy and meant to be rolled. Just work quickly, using foil to help you as you go.

YIELD · ONE 8-INCH-LONG JELLY ROLL

5 tablespoons all-purpose flour

½ teaspoon baking powder

½ teaspoon cornstarch

3 tablespoons milk (I use 2%)

1 tablespoon unsalted butter

5 tablespoons granulated sugar

2 large eggs, at room temperature

**⅓ cup favorite jam
(I use raspberry or plum)**

Powdered sugar, for serving

Preheat the oven to 350°F.

Use an 8-inch square baking pan with sharp corners for this recipe; I don't recommend ceramic bakeware because the edges are rounded, and the cake won't roll evenly. Trim parchment paper to fit the bottom of the pan perfectly by flipping the pan over and tracing the bottom of the pan onto the paper. Place the parchment in the bottom of the brownie pan. Do not grease the pan.

In a medium bowl, sift together the flour, baking powder, and cornstarch twice. Be careful not to lose any of the flour in the sifting.

Combine the milk and butter in a small microwave-safe bowl, and heat on high for about 20 seconds, just until steaming hot. Set aside.

In a medium bowl, combine the granulated sugar and eggs. Beat with an electric mixer on high speed until it has the consistency of softened whipped cream. This can take anywhere from 5 to 10 minutes.

Add one-third of the flour mixture to the egg mixture. Using a rubber spatula, gently fold the mixture together. (Proper folding technique is to slice down the middle with the spatula, and then sweep the sides of the bowl.) Add another third of the flour mixture, and repeat the folding process. Take your time; don't rush it. Finally, add the remaining flour and fold in very well.

Reheat the butter mixture for 15 seconds in the microwave, until steamy hot. Pour all of it at once into the flour mixture and fold it together.

Scrape the batter into the prepared pan. Bake for 20 minutes, or until a toothpick inserted in the center comes out clean.

Remove the pan from the oven, and let it cool on a cooling rack for 10 minutes. After 10 minutes, run a butter knife around the edges of the cake to release it from the pan, and then gently tip the cake out onto the cooling rack, bottom facing up.

Let the cake cool completely before gently peeling off the parchment paper. A slight coating of cake may stick to it—it's fine.

Once the cake has completely cooled, transfer the cake to a piece of aluminum foil. Beginning with the edge closest to you, roll the first inch of the cake tightly and firmly. Squeeze the roll together all along the edges with your hands, and use the foil to keep rolling up the cake. The foil will stay on the outside of the cake, but it will help you roll it tightly. When you get to the end, squeeze the cake roll together in your hands to ensure a tight roll. Twist the ends of the foil closed, and refrigerate the cake for at least 4 hours. You could do this 1 day in advance.

Before serving, unroll the cake gently and spread it with the jam. Roll it back up, sprinkle with powdered sugar, slice, and serve.

Maple Bacon Cupcakes

Maple bacon cupcakes are soft, tender cupcakes with a small amount of bacon grease in the batter. The frosting is maple flavored and crowned with a candied maple bacon piece. It's like your favorite donut, but in cupcake form!

YIELD · 10 CUPCAKES

FOR THE CUPCAKES
5 slices of bacon

**⅔ cup maple syrup, plus
2 tablespoons more for bacon pieces**

**3 tablespoons unsalted
butter, melted**

1 large egg

1 cup all-purpose flour

1 teaspoon baking powder

¼ teaspoon salt

½ cup whole milk

First, make the bacon: Cut the bacon slices in half to make 10 equal pieces and place them in a skillet, not touching each other. Turn the heat to medium and cook the bacon, flipping often, until it's cooked all the way through and just starting to turn crisp around the edges, 7 to 10 minutes.

When the bacon is done, turn the heat off. Pour off the bacon grease and reserve 1 tablespoon for the cupcakes. Leave the bacon in the pan.

Drizzle 2 tablespoons of maple syrup over the bacon slices and turn the heat back on to low. Bring the mixture to a simmer, allowing the bacon pieces to cook in the maple syrup and become sticky, 4 to 5 minutes. Remove the bacon pieces from the skillet and set aside to cool.

Preheat the oven to 325°F and place 10 cupcake liners in a muffin pan.

In a medium bowl, add 3 tablespoons of the melted butter, the rest of the maple syrup, and egg to the bowl and whisk very well until well blended.

Whisk in the reserved 1 tablespoon of bacon grease.

Sprinkle the flour, baking powder, and salt evenly over the mixture in the bowl. Whisk in the flour while slowly pouring in the milk. Whisk until combined.

Divide the batter evenly between the 10 cupcake liners.

Bake for 19 to 20 minutes, or until a cake tester comes out clean. Once the cupcakes are cool, you can make the maple buttercream.

FOR THE MAPLE BUTTERCREAM

7 tablespoons unsalted butter, softened

1 cup powdered sugar

2 to 3 tablespoons maple syrup

Big pinch of salt

MAKE THE FROSTING: Beat together the frosting ingredients using an electric mixer. If the mixture seems too stiff, drizzle in an extra tablespoon of maple syrup until it's soft and fluffy.

Scrape the buttercream into a piping bag fitted with a round tip. Decorate the cupcakes with the buttercream by making one large dollop, followed by another smaller dollop, right on top. Decorate each cupcake with a piece of candied bacon and serve.

Small Coconut Cake

This small-batch coconut cake recipe makes a 6-inch mini cake that is so festive for the holidays or a small birthday celebration. This cake is made with coconut milk, coconut oil, and coconut flakes for the maximum amount of coconut flavor!

YIELD · ONE 6-INCH CAKE

FOR THE CAKE

4 tablespoons (½ stick) unsalted butter, at room temperature

2 tablespoons unrefined coconut oil

½ cup granulated sugar

½ teaspoon coconut extract

1 large egg

¾ cup all-purpose flour

⅛ teaspoon salt

½ teaspoon baking soda

½ cup sweetened coconut flakes

¼ cup canned light coconut milk (well shaken)

FOR THE FROSTING

1 tablespoon unsalted butter, at room temperature

1 tablespoon unrefined coconut oil

3 ounces cream cheese, softened

¼ teaspoon coconut extract

2 cups powdered sugar

Roughly ⅓ cup (sweetened coconut flakes (more or less, to taste)

Preheat the oven to 350°F and line a 6-inch round cake pan with parchment paper on the bottom. Give everything a spritz with a coconut oil cooking spray, just to be safe.

In a large bowl, beat together the butter, coconut oil, and sugar until creamy, about 1 minute.

Add the coconut extract and egg and beat until combined.

Sprinkle the flour, salt, baking soda, and coconut flakes evenly over the top.

Start to beat everything together while streaming in the coconut milk.

Beat until fully combined (but be careful not to overmix).

Scrape the mixture into the prepared pan, place the pan on a small baking sheet, and bake for 36 to 38 minutes.

Use a toothpick to ensure it's done. Let the cake cool in the pan on a wire rack, and when it's cool enough to touch, tip it out and peel off the parchment paper.

TO MAKE THE FROSTING: Beat together the butter, coconut oil, cream cheese, and coconut extract.

Start adding the powdered sugar while beating slowly.

Toast the coconut: Place it in a dry skillet and stir frequently over low heat until it's nicely browned. I like it almost crispy because it will soak in the frosting and soften again. Beat the toasted coconut into the frosting. Frost the cake and serve.

Zucchini Cake

I figured we all need a good zucchini cake in our files. This is especially true when a summer vacation coincides with an epic period of zucchini production. Yes, I'm speaking from experience here.

I used coconut sugar for this cake and maple syrup for the frosting. The frosting isn't as sweet as typical cream cheese frosting, but I like it better. (If you want to, add ½ cup of powdered sugar.)

After you grate the zucchini, place it on several sheets of paper towel, let it rest for about 5 minutes, and then try to squeeze as much moisture from it as you can by pressing down on it.

YIELD • ONE 8-INCH CAKE

FOR THE CAKE
1¼ cups all-purpose flour

2 teaspoons ground cinnamon

½ teaspoon ground nutmeg

½ teaspoon ground ginger

½ teaspoon fine sea salt

½ teaspoon baking powder

½ teaspoon baking soda

½ cup vegetable oil

½ cup unsweetened applesauce

1 teaspoon vanilla extract

2 eggs

1 cup coconut sugar

1 cup shredded zucchini, drained and patted dry

FOR THE FROSTING
8 ounces cream cheese

½ teaspoon vanilla

¼ cup maple syrup

Preheat the oven to 350°F. Butter or spray an 8-inch square baking pan with cooking spray and set aside.

In a bowl, combine flour, spices, salt, baking powder, and baking soda.

In a separate bowl, combine oil, applesauce, vanilla, eggs, and coconut sugar. Add to the dry ingredients and mix well.

Add the shredded zucchini and stir until thoroughly combined.

Pour the batter into the prepared pan.

Bake for 30 to 35 minutes or until a toothpick inserted near the center comes out clean. Cool on a wire rack.

Meanwhile, to make the frosting, in a small bowl, beat the cream cheese, maple syrup, and vanilla until smooth and creamy.

When the cake is completely cool, frost it and serve.

Personal Pineapple Upside-Down Cakes

Another excellent contender for my birthday. Caramelized fruit on top of a buttermilk cake always wins my heart. If you don't want to buy a jar of maraschino cherries just for this cake, you can leave them out entirely, or substitute a beautiful pecan half. Please note that this recipe calls for much larger 10-ounce ramekins, not the standard 6-ounce ramekins.

YIELD · 2 INDIVIDUAL CAKES

FOR THE PINEAPPLE TOPPING
2 tablespoons unsalted butter, plus more for ramekins

2 teaspoons granulated sugar

3 tablespoons light brown sugar

4 pineapple rings from an 8-ounce can (usually each can has only 4 slices)

1 halved maraschino cherry

FOR THE CAKES
3 tablespoons unsalted butter, at room temperature

2 tablespoons + 2 teaspoons granulated sugar

½ teaspoon vanilla extract

¼ teaspoon almond extract

1 large egg

½ cup all-purpose flour

Pinch of salt

¾ teaspoon baking powder

⅓ cup buttermilk

TO MAKE THE TOPPING: Preheat the oven to 350°F and butter and sugar two 10-ounce ramekins with 1 teaspoon of granulated sugar each.

In a small skillet over medium-low heat, melt the brown sugar and the remaining 2 tablespoons of butter. When the sugar is melted, divide the mixture between the two ramekins.

Place one pineapple ring in the center of each ramekin. Slice up the remaining rings and arrange them around the whole ring to cover the entire bottom of the ramekin. Place one cherry half in the center of each middle ring, with the flat side facing down. Set aside while making the cake batter.

TO MAKE THE CAKES: In a medium bowl, using an electric mixer on medium speed, beat together the butter and sugar. Add the vanilla and almond extract, then the egg, mixing well. Add the flour, salt, and baking powder. Beat well. Finally, beat in the buttermilk.

Divide the batter evenly between the prepared ramekins. Bake for 30 minutes.

Let cool for 10 to 15 minutes before inverting onto plates and serving while still warm.

Gingerbread Cake + Lemon Glaze

Ahhh, gingerbread, chai, and warm spices—they're kinda my thing. This is probably because I'm always cold. My pantry is always stocked with spices. But I should admit: I don't just make this spicy-sweet gingerbread cake when the weather is chilly. I think the bright lemon glaze on top makes it perfectly acceptable for warm months, too.

YIELD · ONE 6-INCH CAKE

FOR THE CAKE
¾ cup + 2 tablespoons all-purpose flour

1½ teaspoons ground ginger

1 teaspoon cinnamon

Pinch of ground cloves

⅛ teaspoon fine sea salt

½ teaspoon baking soda

¼ cup canola oil

2 tablespoons unsalted butter, melted

1 large egg

¼ cup brown sugar

3 tablespoons molasses

FOR THE GLAZE
Juice of ½ lemon

¾ cup powdered sugar

Preheat the oven to 350°F and thoroughly grease a 6-inch round cake pan.

In a small bowl, whisk together the flour, ginger, cinnamon, cloves, salt, and baking soda.

In a separate bowl, whisk together the oil, melted butter, egg, brown sugar, and molasses. Whisk very well until homogenized; it will take a while to blend the egg and molasses together.

Stir the wet and dry ingredients together, then pour the mixture into the prepared cake pan.

Bake for 30 to 33 minutes until an inserted toothpick comes out clean. The cake may have a slight divot in the center.

Let the cake cool in the pan, and then tilt it out onto a serving plate.

Whisk together the lemon juice and powdered sugar to make the glaze. Pour it over the cake and serve.

Pecan Pie Cheesecake

After the publishing of my first cookbook, I had the pleasure of being asked to bake a few desserts for two on the *Today Show* one morning. I was beyond excited, and chatted back and forth with the producer several times before going on air. She asked a lot of questions about the person who eats the other half of my desserts for two, and I shared the story of how I met my husband. Little did I know, that embarrassing story would be the first thing said on air before my segment.

My husband had attempted to make a pecan pie cheesecake to impress me at a work party, but it was a big flop. It slid all over the plate and was raw in the middle. I still tease him about it to this day, but now, we eat this version of pecan pie cheesecake. Much better.

YIELD · ONE 6-INCH
CHEESECAKE

FOR THE CRUST
1 cup vanilla wafer crumbs
(about 30 cookies, crushed)

1 tablespoon light brown sugar

2½ tablespoons unsalted
butter, melted

FOR THE PECAN PIE FILLING
⅓ cup granulated sugar

¼ cup dark corn syrup

2 tablespoons unsalted butter

1 large egg

¾ cup chopped pecans

1 tablespoon bourbon whiskey

Preheat the oven to 350°F and spray a 6-inch mini cheesecake springform pan with cooking spray.

TO MAKE THE CRUST: In a medium bowl, combine the cookie crumbs, brown sugar, and butter. Stir until well mixed. Press the crumbs firmly into the bottom of the springform pan and halfway up the sides. Bake for 8 minutes, and then remove the pan from the oven. Turn down the oven temperature to 325°F.

TO MAKE THE PECAN PIE FILLING: In a 2-quart saucepan over medium heat, combine all the ingredients for the filling, except the whiskey. Bring to a boil, lower the heat to maintain a simmer, and then simmer until thickened, 8 to 10 minutes. Just a reminder: A simmer is when small bubbles form around the edges of the pan. If you cook this mixture at anything higher, it will harden like candy.

Remove the pecan pie filling from the heat, and stir in the bourbon. Set this mixture aside to cool slightly.

continues

FOR THE CHEESECAKE FILLING

8 ounces cream cheese, softened (see Tip)

⅓ cup light brown sugar

1 tablespoon all-purpose flour

1 large egg

½ teaspoon vanilla extract

2 tablespoons unsalted butter, melted

TO MAKE THE CHEESECAKE FILLING: In a medium bowl, beat together all the cheesecake ingredients until very well mixed.

Pour the pecan pie mixture over the crust, followed by the cheesecake mixture. Spread the cheesecake mixture to the edges of the pan with a small spatula. Ensure the cheesecake mixture is flat and evenly distributed.

Bake the cheesecake on a small baking sheet for 35 to 41 minutes. The cheesecake is done when only the center of it lightly jiggles when gently shaken. A small amount of butter may leak outside your springform pan, but it's fine.

When the cheesecake comes out of the oven, it will be slightly puffy. Place it next to the oven to cool; drastic temperature changes cause cracks in cheesecakes. Let the cheesecake cool gently. It will deflate, but it will turn into a perfectly flat cheesecake. Place in the fridge for at least 6 hours before unmolding and serving.

TIP: People ask me all the time whether they really have to let ingredients like butter or cream cheese come to room temperature before baking. The answer is a resounding YES. I can't stress it enough. If your cream cheese is cold, it will not blend properly and you will see white chunks in your final product. To speed up the softening time, slice the cream cheese and let it sit at room temperature on a plate until it feels slightly cooler than room temperature. Your finger should easily leave an indentation. Or place it (still in the wrapper) in a bowl of warm water for a few minutes.

Tres Leches Cake

The first year I moved to California, I met my best friend, Esther. She made me a Tres Leches cake for my birthday that year, and it's been my go-to birthday cake ever since—a soft milk cake drenched in sweet milk and topped with whipped cream. What's not to love? I hear it's great with strawberries on top, but I never have the patience to garnish the cake. I eat it straight away!

YIELD • ONE 6-INCH CAKE

FOR THE CAKE

½ cup all-purpose flour

¾ teaspoon baking powder

1 large egg, separated

⅛ teaspoon cream of tartar

½ cup granulated sugar

¼ cup half-and-half

TO MAKE THE CAKE: Preheat the oven to 350°F and position a rack in the middle of the oven. Grease a 6-inch round cake pan with cooking spray.

In a small bowl, sift together the flour and baking powder. Set aside.

In a medium bowl, using an electric mixer with superclean beaters on high speed, whip the egg white and cream of tartar until soft peaks form. While continuing to beat, stream in the sugar about 1 tablespoon at a time. Next, beat in the egg yolk.

Fold one-third of the flour mixture into the egg white mixture, using a rubber spatula. Add 2 tablespoons of the half-and-half and other half of the egg white mixture and continue to fold. Add another third of the flour mixture, and fold in. Add the remaining 2 tablespoons of half-and-half. Finally, fold in the last of the flour mixture.

Pour the batter into the prepared cake pan. Bake for 21 to 23 minutes, or until a toothpick inserted into the center comes out clean.

Let the cake cool in the pan for 10 minutes, and then run a knife around the edge of the pan to release it. Tilt the cake out upside down onto a serving plate.

continues

FOR THE TOPPING

½ cup half-and-half

⅔ cup sweetened condensed milk

FOR THE WHIPPED CREAM FROSTING

½ cup heavy whipping cream

2 tablespoons powdered sugar

TO MAKE THE TOPPING: Whisk together the half-and-half and condensed milk. Use a toothpick to poke holes all over the cake. Drizzle the topping over the cake slowly, and let it sink in. Cover the cake and refrigerate for at least 4 hours before frosting.

TO MAKE THE FROSTING: In a medium bowl, using an electric mixer on high speed, whip the cream and powdered sugar together until soft peaks form. Frost the cake and serve.

Cheesecake in a Loaf Pan

I'm having the hardest time deciding the serving size of this small cheesecake made in a loaf pan. I think just how much cheesecake you can eat is personal. A personal accomplishment, if you ask me, but nevertheless, the answer varies.

The way I slice it into little triangles, you will get five smaller-than-average slices of cheesecake. Can you eat two? Can you eat three? Or do you serve this at a dinner party and give each guest one small slice? I've done all three.

YIELD • 2 GENEROUS SERVINGS

FOR THE CRUST
8 graham cracker sheets

2 tablespoons unsalted butter, melted

1 tablespoon granulated sugar

FOR THE FILLING
2 (8-ounce) packages cream cheese, at room temperature

½ cup granulated sugar

1 large egg, beaten

1 teaspoon vanilla extract

1 teaspoon fresh lemon juice

FOR SERVING
4 ounces chopped chocolate

2 teaspoons coconut oil

Preheat the oven to 325°F and line a loaf pan with parchment paper. It doesn't have to cover every side—just the two longest sides.

In a small food processor (or plastic zip-top bag), crush the graham crackers into crumbs. Add the melted butter and sugar, and stir/mix until combined.

Press the crumbs into the loaf pan and bake for 25 minutes until lightly golden brown.

Meanwhile, beat together the cream cheese and sugar with an electric mixer on medium speed until light and fluffy. Beat in the egg, followed by the vanilla and lemon juice.

Pour the cheesecake mixture over the crust.

Lower the oven to 300°F and bake the cheesecake for 30 to 40 minutes, until the entire surface is set and not sticky. It will have a slightly golden yellow hue. An inserted toothpick should not come out wet with batter. Place the cheesecake in the fridge for at least 4 hours (or overnight) before serving.

Let the cheesecake cool near the oven (drastic temperature changes cause cracks). Once fully cooled, move to the refrigerator for at least 4 hours.

When ready to serve, melt the chocolate and coconut oil in a double boiler. Alternatively, set a microwave to 50 percent power and heat the chocolate and coconut oil in 30-second intervals, stirring between each, until melted and smooth.

Swirl the chocolate sauce over the cheesecake and serve.

Donut Gooey Butter Cake

Oh, this cake. It's not to be missed. It's a crisp, buttery crust with a gooey vanilla filling and a topping that shatters like the first bite of a glazed donut, I'm not overselling this, I promise.

Gooey butter cake (when not made from a cake mix, and thus approximately a thousand times better) is two wet batters poured on top of each other and baked. There are yeast versions out there, which I love and adore, but this is my favorite.

If you want to take it up a notch (and dirty another dish), try browning the butter first.

YIELD · ONE 8-INCH CAKE

FOR THE BOTTOM LAYER

6 tablespoons (¾ stick) unsalted butter, melted

½ cup granulated sugar

½ cup brown sugar

2 large eggs

¾ teaspoon fine sea salt

1½ cups all-purpose flour

2 teaspoons baking powder

FOR THE TOP LAYER

8 ounces cream cheese, softened

6 tablespoons brown sugar

2 large eggs

1 tablespoon vanilla extract

3½ cups powdered sugar, plus extra for serving

Preheat the oven to 350°F and line an 8-inch square baking pan one direction with parchment paper. Lightly spray the exposed sides of the pan with cooking spray.

Next, make the bottom layer of the cake. In a medium bowl, whisk together the melted butter, granulated sugar, and brown sugar.

Add the eggs and salt and whisk well to combine. Finally, add the flour and baking powder.

Scoop the mixture into the prepared pan and press flat with your hands. It's a bit sticky—flour your fingers to help spread it evenly.

Then wipe out the bowl and start making the top layer of the cake. Add the cream cheese and brown sugar. Beat with an electric mixer on medium speed until light and fluffy, about 1 minute. Add the eggs and vanilla. Beat until combined. Finally, add the powdered sugar and beat until well mixed and smooth.

Pour the top layer onto the bottom layer.

Bake for 50 to 55 minutes, until the center only has a slight jiggle. Don't overbake (or it won't be gooey).

Let cool completely, then refrigerate or freeze until firm enough to cut.

Sprinkle with powdered sugar and serve.

German Chocolate Cupcakes

Chocolate cupcakes with a creamy coconut pecan frosting, also known as German chocolate cupcakes, are the perfect spring dessert. Do not sleep on this creamy coconut pecan frosting for cupcakes.

YIELD · 4 CUPCAKES

FOR THE CUPCAKES
⅓ **cup milk**

¼ **teaspoon white vinegar**

⅓ **cup all-purpose flour**

4 **teaspoons cocoa powder**

¼ **teaspoon baking soda**

¼ **teaspoon baking powder**

4 **teaspoons canola oil**

¼ **teaspoon vanilla extract**

¼ **cup brown sugar**

FOR THE FROSTING
One 5-ounce can evaporated milk

⅓ **cup sugar**

1 **egg yolk**

2 **tablespoons unsalted butter**

¼ **cup chopped pecans**

½ **cup sweetened coconut flakes**

Preheat the oven to 350°F. Line four cups of a muffin pan with paper liners. Gather all ingredients.

Pour the milk into a small bowl. Add the vinegar and let sit while you prepare the rest of the ingredients.

Sift together the flour, cocoa powder, baking soda, and baking powder in a small bowl.

In another bowl, whisk together the oil, vanilla, and brown sugar.

Add the dry ingredients to the oil and brown sugar mixture in two batches, alternating with the milk mixture. Whisk until smooth but try not to overmix.

Divide the batter between the four muffin cups and bake for 15 to 18 minutes, or until a toothpick inserted comes out clean. Let cool on a wire rack.

Next, make the frosting: In a small saucepan, add the evaporated milk, sugar, egg yolk, and butter. Turn the heat to medium-low and cook while stirring until the mixture starts to simmer around the edges of the pan. Lower the heat slightly, then continue to cook while stirring another minute. It will thicken.

Turn off heat and stir in the pecans and coconut flakes. Pour the mixture into a bowl, let cool to room temperature, then refrigerate until ready to serve the cupcakes.

To serve, frost the cupcakes with the chilled frosting. It will be considerably thicker after chilling.

S'mores Baked Alaska

I love using a muffin pan to make individual desserts. This S'mores Baked Alaska is easy: line a few muffin cups with crushed graham crackers, smush your favorite chocolate ice cream on top, and store it in the freezer until you're ready.

The day of, make the marshmallow fluff. When you're ready, remove the ice cream pucks from the muffin pan, place them on a serving plate, cover them with the marshmallow fluff, and torch! Yes, the torch is going to slightly melt the ice cream. It's okay.

YIELD · 4 ALASKAS

4 whole graham cracker sheets

1½ tablespoons unsalted butter, melted

1 pint chocolate ice cream

2½ cups sugar

½ cup light corn syrup

2 large egg whites

¼ teaspoon cream of tartar

Line four muffin cups in a pan with plastic wrap, overlapping as necessary.

Crush the graham crackers into crumbs using a plastic bag or a food processor. You should get about ½ cup of crumbs.

Combine the graham cracker crumbs and the melted butter in a small bowl. Firmly press the crumbs into each muffin cup. Place the pan in the freezer for 30 minutes.

Meanwhile, soften the chocolate ice cream until it's easy to scoop.

Remove the pan from the freezer and smush chocolate ice cream into each of the cups, leveling the surface so that it's flat. Return the pan to the freezer for at least 4 hours, or up to 2 days in advance.

ON SERVING DAY, MAKE THE MARSHMALLOW FLUFF: In a small saucepan, combine 3 tablespoons of water, the sugar, and corn syrup. Stir together gently (try not to splash sugar crystals on the edges of the pan).

Turn the heat to medium-high and bring the mixture to 240°F.

Meanwhile, add the egg whites and the cream of tartar to the bowl of a stand mixer. Beat them until soft peaks form, 3 to 4 minutes.

When the sugar syrup mixture reaches 240°F, immediately remove it from the heat and stream it into the egg whites while mixing on high speed.

Beat on high speed until light and fluffy, 4 to 5 minutes. Let the marshmallow fluff cool completely (4 to 5 hours before serving).

When you want to serve, remove each ice cream puck from the muffin pan and place it on a serving plate and spread with fluff. You can freeze these covered in fluff up to 4 hours, too.

Use a culinary torch to lightly toast the fluff. Serve immediately.

Quick (No-Yeast) Cinnamon Rolls

Easily one of the most popular recipes on my website, and for a good reason: Who doesn't love homemade cinnamon rolls in half the time? To avoid using yeast, these rolls have an almost biscuit-like preparation method. This gives them an ever-so-slightly different flavor than authentic yeast cinnamon rolls, but you won't get any complaints!

YIELD · 4 CINNAMON ROLLS

FOR THE ROLLS
¾ cup all-purpose flour, plus more for dusting

2 tablespoons granulated sugar, divided

½ teaspoon baking powder

¼ teaspoon baking soda

⅛ teaspoon salt

5 tablespoons milk

1 teaspoon cider vinegar

4 tablespoons (½ stick) unsalted butter, melted, divided

3 tablespoons light brown sugar

1 teaspoon ground cinnamon

FOR THE FROSTING
3 ounces cream cheese, softened

⅓ cup powdered sugar

Splash of milk or heavy whipping cream

Preheat the oven to 375°F and spray four cups in a muffin pan with cooking spray or melted unsalted butter.

TO MAKE THE ROLLS: Combine the flour, 1 tablespoon of the granulated sugar, baking powder, baking soda, and salt in a medium bowl.

In a small measuring cup, combine the milk, vinegar, and 2 tablespoons of the melted butter.

Add the wet ingredients to the dry, and stir until a soft dough forms.

Heavily flour a work surface, and pat the dough out into a rectangle about 6 inches long. Use plenty of flour as you go.

Pour the remaining 2 tablespoons of melted butter on top of the dough.

Combine the brown sugar, cinnamon, and remaining 1 tablespoon of granulated sugar. Press this mixture lightly into the butter on top of the dough. Carefully roll up the dough, starting with a long side and rolling away from you. When you get to the end of the dough, pinch the entire seam shut.

Cut the dough into four equal pieces and drop into the greased muffin cups.

Bake for 14 to 15 minutes.

TO MAKE THE FROSTING: Beat together the cream cheese and powdered sugar. If it seems hard to spread, splash in some milk or cream.

Frost the cinnamon rolls when they come out of the oven, and serve.

Coffee Cake Muffins

Because who doesn't want a little bite of cake for breakfast?

FOR THE CRUMB TOPPING

¼ cup lightly packed light brown sugar

1 tablespoon granulated sugar

Pinch of salt

¼ teaspoon ground cinnamon

1 tablespoon unsalted butter, melted

3 tablespoons all-purpose flour

FOR THE MUFFINS

¼ cup canola oil

⅓ cup granulated sugar

Pinch of salt

1 large egg

2 tablespoons heavy whipping cream or sour cream

½ teaspoon vanilla extract

⅓ cup + 1 tablespoon all-purpose flour

⅛ teaspoon baking soda

⅛ teaspoon baking powder

¼ teaspoon ground cinnamon

⅛ teaspoon freshly grated nutmeg

Preheat the oven to 375°F and line four cups in a muffin pan with muffin liners.

TO MAKE THE CRUMB TOPPING: In a small bowl, combine all the topping ingredients and use your fingers to pinch the ingredients together to make large clumps. Set aside.

TO MAKE THE MUFFINS: In a medium bowl, beat together the oil and granulated sugar with an electric mixer on medium speed for 4 minutes. Add the salt, egg, cream, and vanilla and beat for 15 seconds.

Sprinkle the remaining dry ingredients on top, and beat just to combine.

Scoop 1½ tablespoons of the batter into each prepared muffin cup. Top with a spoonful of crumb topping, and then divide the rest of the batter equally among all the muffin cups. Top the batter with the remaining crumb topping.

Bake for 19 to 23 minutes, until a toothpick inserted comes out cleanly and the crumb topping is golden brown.

Maple Syrup Mini Cake

This pretty sprinkled cake is made entirely with maple syrup instead of any other type of sugar. For this reason, I love to use it for babies' first birthday smash cakes. The batter can also be distributed into eight muffin cups to make cupcakes instead.

FOR THE CAKE
3 tablespoons unsalted butter, melted

1 tablespoon neutral oil (grapeseed)

⅔ cup maple syrup

1 large egg

1 cup all-purpose flour

1 teaspoon baking powder

¼ teaspoon fine sea salt

½ cup whole milk

FOR THE COCONUT WHIPPED CREAM
One 14-ounce can coconut cream, refrigerated overnight

1½ tablespoons maple syrup

Rainbow sprinkles, for decorating (optional)

Preheat the oven to 325°F and grease a 6-inch round cake pan.

In a medium bowl, beat with an electric mixer the melted butter and oil.

Stream in the maple syrup and keep beating.

Next, add the egg and beat until combined.

Sprinkle the flour, baking powder, and salt evenly over the batter, and beat just to combine for a few seconds, then add all of the milk at once.

Beat everything until smooth, scraping down the sides of the bowl as you go.

Pour the mixture into the prepared pan and bake for 20 minutes.

To make the coconut cream, you really should refrigerate the bowl and the can of coconut cream overnight.

When the cupcakes are totally cool, make the frosting: Scrape all the coconut cream out of the can and into a cold bowl (do not add the little bit of coconut water or juice in the can—just the thick, white cream).

Beat with an electric mixer on high until light and fluffy. Add the maple syrup and beat to combine.

Taste the frosting; if you want it sweeter, you're going to have to add powdered sugar because any more maple syrup will make it too thin.

Frost the cake, decorate with sprinkles, if using, and serve.

PIES, COBBLERS & PUDDING

Blueberry Mason Jar Lid Pies

Mini pies are fun to serve and eat, but making them can be a bit tedious. I use the lids of mason jars as a makeshift springform pan. The pies are perfectly portioned and pop out immediately.

YIELD • 2 INDIVIDUAL PIES

¾ cup + 2 teaspoons all-purpose flour, divided, plus more for rolling

¼ teaspoon salt

3 tablespoons cold unsalted butter

¼ teaspoon cider vinegar

2 to 3 tablespoons ice water

½ cup frozen blueberries (do not thaw)

½ teaspoon fresh lemon zest (optional)

1 teaspoon fresh lemon juice

1 tablespoon granulated sugar

1 large egg yolk, beaten

Sanding sugar (optional)

You will need two wide-mouth mason jar lids for this recipe. You can substitute four regular mason jar lids. Turn the mason jar lid inserts over so that the rubber part is down. You want to cook the pies on the metal side.

To make the crust, in a small bowl, stir together the ¾ cup of flour and the salt with a fork. Cube the butter into 12 chunks. Add six chunks of butter to the flour mixture and stir gently, and then add the remaining six butter chunks.

Use your fingertips to cream the butter into the flour. Pinch and smear the butter between your fingertips until it's very well incorporated and smaller than peas. The dough will clump when you squeeze it in your hands.

Stir the vinegar into 2 tablespoons of the ice water. Add this to the dough, and stir with a fork. The dough will easily come together into a mass. If the dough still feels too dry, add the extra tablespoon of water. Scoop the dough out onto a piece of plastic wrap, shape it into a disk, and store it wrapped in the fridge for 30 minutes. (If you store the dough for longer than 30 minutes, let it warm up before rolling or it will crack during rolling.)

Preheat the oven to 350°F and line a small sheet pan with parchment paper.

Stir the blueberries, lemon zest, lemon juice, granulated sugar, and remaining 2 teaspoons of flour together in a small bowl. Set aside while you roll out the dough.

Bring the dough out of the fridge, and lightly flour a work surface. Place the dough in the center of the flour, and then flour the top of the dough.

Begin gently rolling out the dough away from you, making a quarter-turn clockwise after every two rolls. This method keeps the dough from sticking to the counter and also creates a perfect circle.

When you have a circle large enough for four mason jar lids, you're ready. Place one mason jar lid ring on the pastry and use a knife to cut a circle of dough ¼ inch larger than the lid. Repeat to make two disks. These are the piecrust bottoms. Then, use the mason jar lid top (not the ring) to cut out two pie tops.

Gently move the piecrust bottoms to the mason jar lids, and press it into place. Scoop half of the blueberry mixture onto each. Top the blueberry mixture with the pie tops. Brush beaten egg yolk very generously on each mini pie. Sprinkle with sanding sugar, if desired.

Bake for 35 to 37 minutes, or until the filling is bubbling and the crust is brown.

Let cool for 5 minutes. To serve, run a knife along the edge of the mason jar ring to release the pies.

Chocolate Caramel Mason Jar Lid Tarts

Mason jar recipes are adorable, and perfect for portion control. Ever since I noticed they mimic little tart pans with removable bottoms, I've been baking up all sorts of treats in them. Play around with the fillings in this recipe—substitute a different type of chocolate if you like, use jam instead of caramel, or try cookies instead of graham crackers. The possibilities are endless and delicious!

YIELD • 4 INDIVIDUAL TARTS

4 graham cracker sheets, broken into pieces

2 teaspoons granulated sugar

2½ tablespoons unsalted butter, melted

2 cups milk chocolate chips

¼ cup heavy whipping cream

2 to 3 teaspoons Salted Caramel Sauce (page 73)

Preheat the oven to 350°F. Place four pint mason jar rings on a small baking sheet. Place the lids with the rubber part facing down.

In a food processor, combine the graham crackers and sugar. Pulse for about 30 seconds, or until finely ground. Stream in the melted butter and continue to pulse. The mixture should appear like wet sand, and it should slightly clump together when squeezed in your hand.

Divide the graham cracker crumbs between the mason jar lids. Use a shot glass to pack in the crumbs and push them up the sides of the ring.

Bake for 10 minutes. Let cool completely on a cooling rack.

Now we're going to melt the chocolate. Bring 1 cup of water to a boil in a small saucepan. Make sure you have a metal bowl that fits over the pan without touching the water. Place the chocolate chips and cream in the bowl, and have it ready next to the stove. Once the water boils, turn off the heat and place the bowl of chocolate and cream over the pan. Stir, stir, stir until the chocolate melts. You may have to turn the heat back on to boil the water again, but I find that if I'm patient while stirring the chocolate, it all melts.

Pour the melted chocolate into the tart shells. Tap the lids gently to get rid of any air bubbles. Let sit for 10 minutes.

Dot drops of caramel sauce onto the surface of the chocolate, and after a few seconds, run a toothpick or knife through the chocolate to swirl it together.

I recommend refrigerating the tarts for a few hours to set the chocolate. However, before serving, let them come back to room temperature—the chocolate is too hard when cold.

The tarts will keep for up to 3 days refrigerated.

Mini Chocolate Cream Pie

This is the recipe that launched my career in food. After tasting my family's recipe for chocolate cream pie and hearing the story about how my grandpa missed this pie so much when he was serving in Pearl Harbor that he ate an entire pan of it upon his homecoming, I knew I had to share the recipe. It was actually the first recipe I ever shared on my blog back in 2010 and I never dreamed it would be the start of my career in food. After one bite, you'll have a hard time deciding if this serves one or two!

YIELD · ONE 6-INCH PIE

FOR THE CRUST

4 whole graham cracker sheets

2½ tablespoons unsalted butter, melted

Pinch of cinnamon

2 teaspoons sugar

FOR THE FILLING

¼ cup sugar

3 tablespoons unsweetened cocoa powder

2½ tablespoons cornstarch

1½ cups milk (I've used 1% and 2% successfully)

1 large egg yolk

1 teaspoon vanilla extract

1 tablespoon unsalted butter

FOR THE WHIPPED CREAM

4 tablespoons heavy whipping cream

2 tablespoons powdered sugar

¼ teaspoon vanilla extract

Chocolate shavings, for garnish (optional)

Preheat the oven to 350°F. Have ready a 6-inch pie pan.

Pulse the graham crackers, melted butter, cinnamon, and sugar in a food processor. Alternatively, you can crush them in a plastic storage bag. Make sure the crumbs are very fine. Press the mixture into the pie pan, using the bottom of a glass or small measuring cup to pack the crumbs firmly. Press the crust up the edges of the pie pan.

Bake the crust on a cookie sheet for 10 minutes. Remove it from the oven and let it cool while you make the chocolate filling.

Sift the sugar, cocoa powder, and cornstarch into a small bowl. Add ½ cup of the milk and whisk vigorously until the mixture is very smooth and free of lumps. Slowly add the rest of the milk while whisking constantly. Finally, whisk in the egg yolk.

Pour the mixture into a small pan and bring it to a simmer over medium heat. Stir the mixture constantly with a wooden spoon, being sure to scrape the corners of the pan with the spoon. Once the mixture starts to thicken and simmer, turn the heat to low and continue cooking for 1 minute. The mixture should be silky and slightly thickened—it will firm up in the crust later. To test the thickness, coat the back of a spoon with the mixture and quickly run your finger through it. If the pudding holds the line, you're good! If it runs back together, it still needs a few minutes of cooking.

Remove the pan from the heat and add the butter. Stir to melt it, then stir in the vanilla. Pour the pudding into the crust. Press plastic wrap against the surface of the pudding and chill in the fridge for at least 4 hours or overnight.

When you're ready to serve the pie, whip the heavy cream, sugar, and vanilla together until a thick whipped cream forms. Spread it evenly on top of the pie, garnish with chocolate shavings, slice, and serve.

Eggnog Bread Pudding

My friend decoded the mystery of making individual portions of bread pudding in ramekins. I'm just here to spread her gospel. I used eggnog as a fun seasonal twist on her recipe.

YIELD · 2 SERVINGS

2 large eggs

6 tablespoons store-bought eggnog

2 tablespoons granulated sugar, plus extra for sprinkling

1 teaspoon whiskey

¼ teaspoon freshly grated nutmeg, plus extra for serving

2 slices fresh white bread, cubed

Freshly whipped cream, for serving

Preheat the oven to 350°F and line a small baking sheet with foil.

Spray two 6-ounce ramekins with cooking spray.

In a medium bowl, whisk together the eggs, eggnog, 2 tablespoons of the sugar, the whiskey, and the nutmeg.

Add the bread cubes and stir to coat.

Equally divide the mixture between the two ramekins and sprinkle a big pinch of sugar over each one.

Bake for 32 to 35 minutes, until puffed and lightly golden brown.

Serve warm with whipped cream and freshly grated nutmeg.

Raspberry Pick-Up Pie

I call crostatas "pick-up pies." Once baked, you can cut them into four neat slices and enjoy them straight out of hand. Sometimes, a pie craving is just too strong to wait for a plate and fork.

YIELD · ONE 6-INCH MINI PIE

½ cup + 2 teaspoons all-purpose flour, divided, plus more for rolling

5 teaspoons granulated sugar, divided

⅛ teaspoon salt

2 tablespoons cold unsalted butter, diced

¼ teaspoon white vinegar

2 to 3 tablespoons cold water

6 ounces fresh raspberries

Beaten egg yolk, for brushing

Coarse sugar (optional)

Raspberry jam, for serving (optional)

Combine ½ cup of the flour, 1 teaspoon of the granulated sugar, and the salt in a medium bowl. Add the butter, and work it through the dough, using two knives or a pastry blender. The butter should be smaller than peas, and evenly dispersed throughout the dough.

In a small bowl, combine the vinegar with 2 tablespoons of the cold water. Add to the dough, and stir with a fork until a shaggy dough forms. If the dough seems a bit too dry, add up to 1 additional tablespoon of water. Shape the dough into a ball, flatten into a disk, then refrigerate for at least 30 minutes.

Preheat the oven to 375°F and place a piece of parchment paper on a small sheet pan.

Combine the raspberries, remaining 2 teaspoons of flour, and remaining 4 teaspoons of granulated sugar. Set aside.

Remove the dough from the fridge, and flour a surface on which to roll it. Roll the dough into a rough 8-inch circle. Move the dough to the sheet pan. Pile the raspberries in the center of the dough, leaving a 2-inch border all around. Begin to fold up the edges of the dough over the raspberries. The majority of the raspberries will not be covered by the crust.

Brush the edges of the pie with egg yolk, and sprinkle with coarse sugar, if using.

Bake for 35 to 40 minutes. The piecrust will be shiny and golden brown, and the raspberries will slump when done.

Let cool completely before serving. I like to warm raspberry jam in the microwave and brush it on the berries before serving.

Key Lime Pie in a Loaf Pan

My love for key lime pie does not have a limit, so if you put an entire key lime pie in front of me, I will eat the whole pie. So, I scaled down my favorite recipe for key lime pie and bake it in a 9-by-5-inch loaf pan.

Use a shot glass to force the graham cracker crumbs up the sides of the pan so that they hold all of the pie filling.

Note that I've used regular limes in this recipe, but also call for 1 tablespoon of fresh lemon juice to mimic the flavors of a true key lime. However, if you have real key limes, please use them! You need ¼ cup of citrus juice in total.

YIELD • 5 SMALL SLICES OF PIE

FOR THE CRUST
8 whole graham cracker sheets

3 tablespoons unsalted butter, melted

1½ tablespoons granulated sugar

FOR THE FILLING
One 14-ounce can sweetened condensed milk

Juice and zest of 3 limes (3 tablespoons total juice)

1 tablespoon fresh lemon juice

3 large egg yolks

Freshly whipped cream, for serving

Preheat the oven to 350°F.

Line a 9-by-5-inch loaf pan with parchment paper; let the parchment paper overhang the sides to use as handles to lift out the pie once it's baked. Spray the pan with cooking spray.

In a food processor, combine the graham crackers, melted butter, and sugar. Pulse until the crumbs are fine and look like wet sand.

Press the graham cracker crumbs into the pan, and, using a shot glass, press the crust up all sides of the pan by 1 inch. Take your time and press it firmly.

Bake the crust for 10 minutes, then remove it from the oven and let cool. Leave the oven on.

Meanwhile, in a small bowl, whisk together the condensed milk, citrus juices, and egg yolks. Using a microplane grater, grate the zest of 1 lime into the mixture and whisk to combine.

Pour the filling into the crust and slide it back into the oven for 18 to 20 minutes. When the pie is done, it will be slightly jiggly.

Let the pie cool to room temperature, cover it with plastic wrap loosely, and refrigerate it overnight.

When you're ready to serve it, use the parchment paper handles to gently lift out the pie. Slice it into five pieces and serve with whipped cream and extra freshly grated lime zest on top.

Caramel Apple Cheesecake Pie

The first time I had this pie-cheesecake-cobbler mash-up was in apple-picking country outside Lake Tahoe, California. Esther (the same girl who makes me Tres Leches cake for my birthday) led a girls' adventure one weekend, when we picked apples, drank cider, and ate too much pie. I can't tell you a thing about the apples that day, all I remember is this cheesecake tucked into a piecrust topped with apples and crumb topping.

YIELD • ONE 6-INCH PIE

1 recipe pie dough (from 173)

All-purpose flour, for rolling

FOR THE CRUMB TOPPING
¼ cup all-purpose flour

2 teaspoons granulated sugar

¼ teaspoon ground cinnamon

Pinch of freshly grated nutmeg

⅛ teaspoon ground ginger

3 tablespoons unsalted butter, at room temperature

FOR THE FILLING
1 small apple (I prefer Honeycrisp)

¼ teaspoon ground cinnamon

1 teaspoon all-purpose flour

Pinch of salt

Pinch of orange zest

6 ounces cream cheese, softened

½ teaspoon vanilla extract

1 large egg, at room temperature

¼ cup granulated sugar

2 teaspoons cornstarch

FOR SERVING
Salted Caramel Sauce (page 73)

Prepare the piecrust through step 2 of Raspberry Pick-Up Pie on page 173.

Preheat the oven to 375°F.

TO MAKE THE TOPPING: Combine all the ingredients, except the butter, in a small bowl. Mix well. Then, add the butter and mix until the butter is about the size of peas and evenly distributed throughout the entire crumb topping. Set aside.

TO MAKE THE FILLING: Peel, core, and dice your apple into ¼-inch chunks. You should end up with about 1 cup of diced apple.

Place the apple in a medium bowl and toss with the cinnamon, flour, salt, and orange zest.

In another bowl, beat together the cream cheese, vanilla, egg, sugar, and cornstarch. Set aside while you prepare the piecrust.

Roll out the dough on a floured surface until it is a few inches wider than the 6-inch pie pan. Place the dough in the pie pan, fold under the edges, and crimp them decoratively.

Transfer the pie to a small baking sheet and bake in the oven for 10 minutes.

Remove from the oven. If the crust has puffed up, gently push it back down before pouring the cream cheese mixture on top. Add the apple mixture on top, followed by the crumb topping. Bake for 30 to 40 minutes. If the crumbs aren't brown enough, broil for a few minutes. This pie is great at room temperature, or even chilled.

TO SERVE: Drizzle with caramel sauce and serve.

Apple Slab Pie

When it comes to apple desserts, I take a cue from my favorite bakery, Big Sur Bakery, and go heavy on the nutmeg, easy on the cinnamon. Apples have enough flavor to stand on their own, and cinnamon has a way of overpowering them. Nutmeg is the perfect complement.

A few years ago, slab pie became the new trend in pie-eating. And since I would never want your dessert habits to be out of style, I scaled down the slab pie to serve two. A slab pie is typically larger and flatter than a regular pie, all the while cramming in just as much pie flavor. I think you'll love this mini slab pie made in a loaf pan to serve two.

YIELD · 2 SERVINGS

FOR THE CRUST
1 cup + 2 tablespoons all-purpose flour

2 teaspoons granulated sugar

¼ teaspoon salt

5 tablespoons cold unsalted butter

½ teaspoon cider vinegar

4 to 5 tablespoons ice-cold water

FOR THE FILLING
2 medium Granny Smith apples

¼ cup light brown sugar

2 tablespoons granulated sugar, plus more for top

1 tablespoon fresh lemon juice

½ teaspoon ground cinnamon, plus more for top

½ teaspoon freshly grated nutmeg

2 tablespoons all-purpose flour

1 large egg yolk, beaten

Preheat the oven to 350°F and lightly spray a 9-by-5-inch loaf pan with cooking spray.

TO MAKE THE CRUST: In a medium bowl, combine the flour, granulated sugar, and salt. Stir until combined, and then dice the cold butter before adding it to the mixture. Use your fingers or a pastry blender to blend the butter into the flour mixture until it's smaller than peas. It should clump together lightly in your hand when squeezed.

Stir the vinegar and 4 tablespoons of the water into the dough. Stir with a fork until it comes together; if it seems a bit dry, add the final tablespoon of water. Gather the dough into a ball, and press it into a flat disk on a well-floured surface. Cut it roughly in half, with one of the halves being slightly larger.

Roll the larger dough half into an 11-by-7-inch rough rectangle—about the size of the bottom of the loaf pan with an extra inch on all sides. Carefully transfer the dough to the loaf pan and press it into the bottom, but let the excess come up the sides of the pan. Don't stretch the dough up the sides of the pan; just let it naturally rest on the edges.

TO MAKE THE FILLING: Peel and slice the apples. I cut six or seven slices out of each quarter of an apple, and then cut the slices in half once to make them fit into the pan easier. Place the apples in a bowl, stir in the brown sugar, the 2 tablespoons of granulated sugar, and the lemon juice, cinnamon, and nutmeg. Stir very well, and then let rest while you continue.

Roll out the other half of the dough to about the size of the loaf pan on top—an extra ½ inch around the edges is helpful for sealing.

Stir the apples again, and then stir in the flour very well. Pour the apples into the bottom crust, and top with the top crust. As best as you can, use your fingers to push the two edges of the dough together to create a light seal.

Brush the egg yolk on top, and sprinkle the extra granulated sugar and cinnamon on top of the dough before sliding the pan into the oven.

Bake for 45 to 50 minutes, until the edges of the dough are turning golden brown and the juices of the apples are bubbling.

Let cool completely (overnight in the fridge is best) for cutting perfect bars.

Blackberry Cobbler
with Lemon Biscuits

A warm berry cobbler with lemony biscuits on top. Yep, it's exactly as delicious as it sounds.

YIELD · 1 SMALL COBBLER

FOR THE FILLING
12 ounces unsweetened frozen blackberries (do not thaw)

¼ cup granulated sugar

1½ teaspoons fresh lemon juice

¼ teaspoon ground cinnamon

2 tablespoons all-purpose flour

FOR THE LEMON BISCUITS
⅔ cup all-purpose flour

1½ teaspoons baking powder

½ teaspoon salt

1 teaspoon granulated sugar

½ cup heavy whipping cream

Zest of 1 lemon

1 egg yolk, beaten (optional)

TO MAKE THE FILLING: Preheat the oven to 400°F.

Place the blackberries in a small baking dish with a 3- to 4-cup capacity. Sprinkle the sugar, lemon juice, cinnamon, and flour on top. Stir gently to combine.

TO MAKE THE BISCUITS: Combine the flour, baking powder, salt, and sugar in a bowl. Make a well in the center, then pour in the cream and add the lemon zest. Knead until a dough comes together.

Pat the dough into a 6-inch square, and then cut it into nine squares. Scatter the dough pieces on top of the blackberries. Brush the dough with the beaten egg yolk, if using.

Bake for 20 minutes, until the berries are bubbling and the biscuits are browned. Serve warm.

Fresh Peach Cobbler

Fresh peach cobbler made with fresh peaches, Southern style! This fresh peach cobbler for two recipe is Texas style with a thin pancake-like batter; you've got to try it! You'll never go back to any other peach cobbler recipe.

YIELD • 4 SERVINGS

4 tablespoons (½ stick) cold unsalted butter

2 pounds fresh peaches (4 to 6 ripe peaches)

8 tablespoons granulated sugar, divided

2 teaspoons fresh lemon juice

½ teaspoon ground cinnamon

½ cup + 2 tablespoons all-purpose flour

1 teaspoon baking powder

½ cup half and half

½ teaspoon vanilla extract

Preheat the oven to 350°F.

While the oven is preheating, slice the butter into four equal pieces and place it in an 8-inch square baking dish. Place the baking dish in the oven while it preheats but keep an eye on it—don't let the butter brown. Remove the pan from the oven when the butter is fully melted.

Meanwhile, peel the peaches. You can either use a very sharp vegetable peeler or dunk them in boiling water for 30 seconds. Place them in an ice bath immediately after the boiling water, then the skins slip right off. Cut them in half, remove the pits, and slice into six to eight pieces each.

Stir together the peach slices, 2 tablespoons of the sugar, the lemon juice, and cinnamon in a bowl, and set aside while you make the rest.

Whisk together the flour, the remaining 6 table-spoons of sugar, and the baking powder. Lightly stir in the half-and-half and vanilla—small lumps are okay.

Spoon the batter over the melted butter in each baking dish and *do not stir*.

Evenly pour the fruit mixture on top. Bake for 35 to 40 minutes, or until the crust is golden brown.

Strawberry Rhubarb Pie

I most definitely did not grow up on rhubarb pie. In fact, I grew up with my grandpa mowing over my grandma's rhubarb patch, and cursing it when it grew back repeatedly. It seems rhubarb fell out of favor in my family, probably after a bumper-crop year where everyone became tired of eating it. I discovered rhubarb all on my own one day at the farmers' market. How could I resist something so beautiful? Hot pink celery? Sign me up! You could use this recipe for double crust to make almost any fruit pie. You may need to increase or decrease the thickener (cornstarch), depending on the pectin levels of the fruit you're using, but you can hardly go wrong with pie.

FOR THE DOUBLE PIECRUST

**1 cup + 2 tablespoons
all-purpose flour**

2 teaspoons granulated sugar

¼ teaspoon salt

**5 tablespoons cold
unsalted butter, diced**

½ teaspoon cider vinegar

4 to 5 tablespoons ice water

FOR THE FILLING

**1½ cups fresh strawberries,
hulled and diced**

½ cup rhubarb stalks, diced

¼ cup granulated sugar

3 tablespoons cornstarch

1 large egg yolk, beaten

Coarse sugar (optional)

TO MAKE THE DOUBLE PIECRUST: In a medium bowl, combine the flour, sugar, and salt. Add the butter and work it into the flour mixture with your fingertips or a pastry cutter. The butter should be evenly distributed and flecked throughout the flour. Next, add the vinegar to 4 tablespoons of the ice water, and sprinkle it over the flour mixture. Stir with a fork until a dough forms. If needed, add up to 1 additional tablespoon of water until the dough comes together but isn't overly wet. Wrap in plastic wrap and let rest in the fridge for at least 30 minutes.

Preheat the oven to 425°F and position a rack in the lower third of the oven.

TO MAKE THE FILLING: In a medium bowl, combine the fruit with the granulated sugar and cornstarch. Set aside.

Divide the dough roughly in half, with one piece slightly larger. Roll out the slightly larger piece on a floured surface until it's a few inches larger than your 6-inch pie pan. Place it in the pan for the bottom crust, and let it hang over.

Roll out the other half of the dough for the top crust. Roll it about the same size as the pie pan.

Pour the fruit and the juices in the bottom crust, top with the top crust, and crimp the top and bottom crust together, trimming off any excess. Make a few slits in the surface of the pie for ventilation.

Brush the entire crust with the beaten egg yolk, and sprinkle with coarse sugar, if using. Bake for 20 minutes, and then open the oven to let out some of the heat. Turn the oven temperature down to 350°F, and continue to bake until the fruit starts to bubble and ooze out of the slits, about 20 minutes longer.

Let cool completely in the pan; overnight is better. Serve.

Berry-misu

Often, I get asked what my favorite dessert is. I usually answer with "pavlova." That is, until I made this citrus-kissed berry tiramisu. I could eat this dessert anytime and never grow tired of it. It's best, of course, when all the summer berries are fresh, but I've been known to make it with a bag of frozen mixed berries, too. In that case, I defrost the berries, drain off the juice, and replace it with even more Chambord.

If you haven't stumbled across Chambord, or raspberry liqueur, it's worth seeking out. I love a splash in hot chocolate in the winter. Suitable replacements are crème de cassis (blackcurrant liqueur) or Cointreau (orange liqueur).

YIELD · 2 TO 4 SERVINGS

3 cups mixed fresh berries (strawberries, blackberries, blueberries, and raspberries), washed

2 tablespoons Chambord (raspberry liqueur)

4 tablespoons powdered sugar, divided

8 ounces mascarpone cheese, softened

1 medium navel orange

Half a 3-ounce package store-bought soft ladyfingers

Slice the strawberries into bite-size pieces and combine in a bowl with the other berries. Sprinkle the Chambord on the berries and stir to combine.

Stir in 2 tablespoons of the powdered sugar, and let rest for 10 minutes. As the berries sit, they will start to release their juices.

Meanwhile, in a small bowl, stir together the softened mascarpone and the other 2 tablespoons of powdered sugar.

Zest the orange into the mascarpone mixture.

Juice the orange and add it to the mascarpone. Stir very well and set aside.

Place four 4-ounce ramekins (or two larger serving bowls) in front of you.

Place a small scoop of fresh berries on the bottom of each ramekin or bowl.

Place one or two ladyfingers on top of the berries.

Spread a thin layer of the mascarpone mixture on top of the ladyfingers.

Repeat the process: berries, ladyfingers, mascarpone, twice in each dish, ending with the remaining berries on top.

Cover the dishes with plastic wrap and refrigerate for at least 4 hours to let the dessert soften and meld together.

Remove the plastic wrap from the berry-misu about 15 minutes before you plan to serve it to allow the mascarpone mixture to soften.

Mini Raspberry Pies

Arguably the cutest thing you can do with a muffin pan. While these look intricate and complicated, using store-bought refrigerated crust and a pizza dough cutter will set you on your way in no time.

I use raspberries because, with a little almond extract, they make my favorite pie, but any berries you love will work here. Blueberries and orange zest? Concord grapes and vanilla? Go for it!

YIELD · 4 MINI PIES

1 sheet refrigerated, premade piecrust

Butter, for greasing the pan

10 ounces fresh raspberries

3 tablespoons granulated sugar

3 tablespoons all-purpose flour

½ teaspoon almond extract

1 teaspoon lemon juice

1 egg yolk, beaten, for glaze

Coarse sugar (optional)

Remove the dough from the fridge about 15 minutes before you want to bake.

Preheat the oven to 350°F and butter four cups in a muffin pan VERY WELL.

Lightly roll out the dough to make it about ½-inch larger in diameter than it is. You will be cutting out four 5-inch circles and using the scraps for the lattice work.

Cut out 5-inch circles using a glass or a biscuit cutter.

Press a circle of dough into each cup. The circles should come up to the top of the cups, maybe slightly higher.

Gather up the pie dough scraps and roll flat again. Use a pizza wheel to cut 7 tiny strips of dough for each pie (that's 28 strips of dough, each about 4 inches long). Flour them well, pile them on a plate, and place the plate in the fridge while you make the filling.

Combine the fresh raspberries, flour, sugar, almond extract, and lemon juice in a bowl. Stir very well. The raspberries will start to break down.

Divide the raspberry mixture between each cup.

Remove the lattice strips from the fridge and lay four across each mini pie. Carefully (and quickly!), loosely weave in three other strips in the opposite direction. It's not a perfect lattice, but it'll be just fine!

Brush each pie with egg yolk and sprinkle with coarse sugar, if using.

Bake the pies for about 20 minutes, until golden brown and the filling is bubbling.

Let the pies cool for 15 minutes, then run a knife around the edges to loosen them.

Remove the pies from the pan to cool completely on a wire rack (don't let them cool in the pan, as they might stick terribly).

DIY Fruit Tarts

Although hard to believe, there are times when a surplus of fresh fruit doesn't get eaten fast enough in our house. It doesn't happen often, but when it does, I always wrap the extra fruit in pastry dough and sprinkle a little sugar on top. This recipe makes two little fruit tarts. I love that you don't have to have a special baking pan to make such cute little pastries. These "tarts" are really crostatas because the dough is loosely folded around the fruit. I think it goes without saying, but please, use any kind of leftover fruit you have in your house! Any type of stone fruit (pitted, of course), fresh berries, a mix of the two—anything, really! As long as you keep the fruit to around 6 ounces total weight, you'll be fine.

YIELD · 2 TARTS

FOR THE CRUST
½ cup all-purpose flour

1 teaspoon granulated sugar

⅛ teaspoon fine sea salt

2 tablespoons cold
unsalted butter, diced

2 to 3 tablespoons cold water

FOR THE FILLING
6 ounces fresh fruit (e.g. 1 small peach, peeled and sliced + a handful of fresh blueberries)

4 teaspoons granulated sugar, plus extra for sprinkling

Zest of ½ lemon

1 large egg yolk, beaten

FOR SERVING
2 scoops vanilla ice cream

Preheat the oven to 375°F.

FIRST, MAKE THE CRUST: Combine the flour, sugar, and salt in a small bowl. With your fingertips, work the cold, diced butter into the flour mixture.

When the butter is evenly dispersed and about the size of rice grains, add 2 tablespoons of cold water to the dough. Stir until a shaggy dough forms. If there are stray bits of flour at the bottom of the bowl, or if the dough seems dry, add the remaining tablespoon of water.

Gather the dough into a ball, wrap it in plastic wrap, and press it into a flat disk.

Refrigerate the dough disk for 30 minutes.

Meanwhile, prep your fruit by washing, peeling, slicing, and/or pitting it, whatever you need to do depending on the fruit you're working with.

Combine the fruit with the 4 teaspoons of sugar and lemon zest. (No matter which fruits I use, I always include the lemon zest because I find it makes all the flavors pop.) Stir to combine.

Divide the chilled dough in half and roll out two 5-inch circles.

Move each circle to a baking pan.

EASY TIP: You can substitute store-bought piecrust for the tart dough. Use a 5-inch biscuit cutter to cut out two rounds of dough from 1 sheet of piecrust.

Evenly divide the fruit into the middle of each dough circle. Using your fingers, carefully pick up the edges of the dough and fold it over the fruit by about 1 inch. See the photo for reference.

Brush the egg yolk on the edges of the crust, sprinkle with sugar, and bake for 25 to 30 minutes.

Let the tarts cool slightly, then serve each with a scoop of vanilla ice cream on top.

Mixed Berry Crostini

You and I are filing this under "healthy and light" desserts, but really, no one will be thinking that as they eat them.

When the berries are appearing at your farmers' markets (and the summer sun is beating down on your back), grab all the berries you can. Snag a whole wheat baguette and some local ricotta cheese. At home, we're going to stir some honey and orange zest into the ricotta cheese, slice up the baguette, and pile the berries on top.

This is the kind of recipe you can easily adapt to serve 2 or 20. My local bread shop carries a mini whole wheat baguette that I love, but if you have a large baguette, freeze the extra slices and pull them out as needed.

8 slices (½ inch thick) whole wheat baguette

½ cup whole milk ricotta cheese

Zest of 1 orange

¼ teaspoon vanilla extract

1 to 2 tablespoons local honey (to taste)

1½ cups fresh fruit (cherries, berries, or a mix)

Place the slices of baguette on a small baking sheet and slide into a low oven, just to warm the slices through.

Meanwhile, stir together the ricotta, orange zest, vanilla, and honey. Taste and adjust to your own liking and sweetness level.

When the bread is just warm, remove it from the oven, slather each slice with the flavored ricotta, and top with fresh fruit.

To serve, drizzle extra honey on top so that it's messy. You can't eat dessert without getting a little messy.

Sweet Tea Lemonade Pie

If there ever was a pie that begged to be packed in a picnic basket and carried to the nearest beach, this would be it. This pie is modeled after the classic lemon icebox pie. I slide mine in the oven for a few minutes just to ensure it sets perfectly.

YIELD • ONE 6-INCH PIE

20 vanilla wafers

2½ tablespoons unsalted butter, melted

¼ cup water

1 small black tea bag

2 large egg yolks

7 ounces sweetened condensed milk

Zest of 1 lemon

3 tablespoons fresh lemon juice

¼ cup heavy whipping cream

1 tablespoon powdered sugar

Lemon slices, for garnish

First, preheat the oven to 350°F and have ready a 6-inch pie pan.

In a food processor, pulse the vanilla wafers until fine crumbs form. Add the melted butter, and pulse again until it just comes together.

Pour the crumbs into the pie pan, and press them firmly up the sides and on the bottom of the pan. Bake on a small baking sheet for 10 minutes.

Meanwhile, boil the water in the microwave (it should only take 45 seconds or so on high). Once boiling, remove from the microwave and add the tea bag. Let steep for 5 minutes. Remove the tea bag and squeeze it gently to get as much tea out of it as possible. You will have slightly less than ¼ cup of tea.

Whisk together the egg yolks, condensed milk, lemon zest, lemon juice, and tea. Pour into the parbaked piecrust. Bake for another 15 minutes.

Let set in the fridge at least 4 hours, or overnight. Before serving, whip the cream and powdered sugar until soft peaks form. Serve with lemon slices.

Strawberry Skillet Cobbler

Think of this as strawberry shortcake, made all in one pan. Just add whipped cream on top before serving. Or serve it right out of the oven with ice cream, like a cobbler. No matter how you serve it, this springtime dessert will be your favorite way to enjoy strawberries. If berries aren't in season, no problem; just use frozen berries.

The 8-inch skillet that I use for this cobbler for two is most likely the smallest skillet that comes in a pots and pans set.

YIELD · ONE 8-INCH COBBLER

1 pound frozen strawberries

2 tablespoons granulated sugar, plus more for sprinkling

Zest and juice of 1 small lemon

2 tablespoons cornstarch

Freshly grated nutmeg, for sprinkling

FOR THE BISCUIT DOUGH
¾ cup all-purpose flour

¾ teaspoon baking powder

¼ teaspoon baking soda

Pinch of salt

3 tablespoons cold unsalted butter

¼ cup milk

Preheat the oven to 400°F.

Pour the frozen strawberries in an 8-inch skillet. Add the sugar, lemon zest, and lemon juice, and place over medium-low heat. Bring to a simmer just to release some of the juices and slightly defrost the berries. Do not overcook. Remove from the heat, and stir in the cornstarch.

TO MAKE THE BISCUIT DOUGH: Combine the flour, baking powder, baking soda, and salt in a small bowl. Dice the butter, and add it to the bowl. Use your fingertips or a pastry blender to blend the butter into the flour mixture. The butter should be evenly distributed and smaller than peas. Add the milk, and stir until a shaggy dough forms.

Dollop the dough in five large clumps over the berries, then sprinkle with sugar and nutmeg. Bake for 18 to 20 minutes, until the berries are bubbling and the biscuits have browned.

Derby Pie

Derby pie is really just an improved version of pecan pie. Along with the usual suspects in pecan pie, Derby pie has bourbon and chocolate. It sounds like an upgrade to me!

**FOR THE CLASSIC SINGLE
PIECRUST**

**1 cup all-purpose flour,
plus more for rolling**

2 teaspoons granulated sugar

¼ teaspoon salt

**4 tablespoons (½ stick) cold
unsalted butter, diced**

½ teaspoon cider vinegar

3 to 5 tablespoons ice water

FOR THE FILLING

¼ cup semisweet chocolate chips

½ cup chopped pecans

¼ cup dark corn syrup

2 tablespoons granulated sugar

2 tablespoons light brown sugar

2 large eggs

1 tablespoon unsalted butter, melted

½ teaspoon cornmeal

¼ teaspoon vanilla extract

¼ teaspoon salt

1 tablespoon bourbon

TO MAKE THE PIECRUST: In a medium bowl, combine the flour, sugar, and salt. Add the butter and work it into the flour mixture with your fingertips or a pastry cutter. The butter should be evenly distributed and flecked throughout the flour. Stir the vinegar into 3 tablespoons of ice water, and then add this to the flour mixture. Stir with a fork to combine. If needed, add up to 2 additional tablespoons of water until the dough comes together but isn't overly wet. It should clump together in your hands when squeezed. Wrap in plastic wrap and let rest in the fridge for at least 30 minutes.

Preheat the oven to 325°F and position a rack in the center of the oven.

Roll out the dough on a floured surface until it is a few inches wider than a 6-inch pie pan. Place the dough in the pie pan, fold under the edges, and crimp them decoratively.

TO MAKE THE FILLING: Sprinkle the chocolate chips and pecans on the piecrust.

In a small saucepan, combine the corn syrup, granulated sugar, and brown sugar. Stir continuously while bringing to a boil. Let it maintain a hard boil (when you can't stir out the boil) for 2 minutes. Remove from the heat, and let cool slightly.

In a separate medium bowl, whisk together the eggs, melted butter, cornmeal, vanilla, and salt. Slowly stream in the boiled syrup mixture, whisking constantly to prevent curdling. Add the bourbon and stir well. Pour the mixture into the piecrust (on top of the pecans and chocolate chips).

Bake on a sheet pan for 45 to 50 minutes. The filling will puff up and will not jiggle when done. Let cool completely before slicing.

Black-Bottom Peanut Butter Pie

This creamy peanut butter pie with a secret chocolate layer is the stuff of which dreams are made.

3 graham cracker sheets

2 tablespoons unsalted, roasted peanut halves

¼ cup + 2 teaspoons granulated sugar, divided

Pinch of salt

2½ tablespoons unsalted butter, melted

½ cup chocolate chips

2 tablespoons cornstarch

½ cup heavy whipping cream, divided

¾ cup milk

½ teaspoon vanilla extract

¼ cup creamy peanut butter

2 teaspoons powdered sugar

Extra peanuts, for garnish

Preheat the oven to 350°F and have ready a 6-inch pie pan.

In a food processor, combine the graham crackers, peanuts, 2 teaspoons of the granulated sugar, and salt. Pulse until finely ground. (Alternatively, you could crush everything in a plastic bag.) Next, add the melted butter. Pulse to combine.

Press the crumbs into the bottom of the pie pan and halfway up the sides, and bake on a small sheet pan for 12 minutes.

When the piecrust comes out of the oven, distribute the chocolate chips over the bottom.

Meanwhile, combine the remaining ¼ cup of granulated sugar and cornstarch in a small bowl. Slowly stream in ¼ cup of the cream while constantly whisking. Once everything is fully dissolved, slowly add the milk while whisking. Pour the mixture into a small saucepan.

Cook over medium heat until the mixture comes to a simmer and thickens. It should have a consistency like runny pudding.

Remove from the heat, and stir in the vanilla and peanut butter. Pour this mixture over the chocolate chips in the piecrust.

Let set in the fridge for at least 4 hours. I don't cover mine because I like the bit of skin that forms, but if you'd rather not have a skin on top, press plastic wrap directly on the surface of the pie before refrigerating.

Before serving, in a medium bowl, using an electric mixer on high speed, beat the remaining ¼ cup of cream until soft peaks form. Beat in the powdered sugar. Spread over the pie, and garnish with the extra peanuts.

Buttermilk Pie

Buttermilk pie is a comforting vanilla custard pie with the tang of buttermilk. I don't think I could ever tire of it. It's great in the summertime with fresh strawberries, and lovely in the winter with warm, poached fruit. But don't relegate it to dessert only—it's lovely for breakfast with chicory coffee, too.

YIELD · ONE 6-INCH PIE

1 recipe pie dough (page 173)

1 tablespoon all-purpose flour, plus more for rolling

½ cup granulated sugar

1 large egg

⅓ cup buttermilk

3 tablespoons unsalted butter, melted

Zest of ½ lemon

1 tablespoon fresh lemon juice

½ teaspoon vanilla extract

Whipped cream, for serving (optional)

Prepare the piecrust through step 2 of Raspberry Pick-Up Pie on page 173.

Preheat the oven to 350°F.

Roll out the dough on a floured surface until it is a few inches wider than the 6-inch pie pan. Place the dough in the pie pan, fold under the edges, and crimp them decoratively.

In a medium bowl, stir together all the remaining ingredients, except the whipped cream. Pour into the crust. Bake for 30 to 35 minutes—the edges will be set but the middle will have a slight jiggle—it will thicken as it cools.

I like this pie chilled, so I chill it for at least 4 hours before serving with whipped cream.

Pumpkin Spice Tiramisu

I'm a firm believer that tiramisu needs to make a comeback. Not only is it easy to make, it's no-bake, too!

YIELD · 2 SERVINGS

¾ cup boiling water

1 tablespoon (heaping) instant espresso powder

1 tablespoon dark rum

8 ounces mascarpone cheese, softened

½ cup canned pure pumpkin puree

⅔ cup + 2 tablespoons powdered sugar, divided

1 teaspoon pumpkin pie spice, plus more for dusting

12 ladyfingers (½ package)

½ cup heavy whipping cream

In a shallow bowl, stir together the boiling water, espresso powder, and rum. Have ready a 1-quart casserole or similarly sized dish.

In a small bowl, stir together the mascarpone, pumpkin, ⅔ cup of the powdered sugar, and teaspoon of pumpkin pie spice. Set aside.

Dunk each ladyfinger in the espresso mixture, and place six of the ladyfingers in a single layer in the casserole dish.

Spread half of the pumpkin mixture on top. Repeat with the remaining ladyfingers and pumpkin filling.

Cover and chill for at least 4 hours, or overnight.

Before serving, whip together the cream and the remaining 2 tablespoons of powdered sugar. Spread on top of the tiramisu, and dust with extra pumpkin pie spice, if desired.

Strawberry Mousse

Have you ever dipped a strawberry in sour cream and then rolled it in brown sugar? That's what this reminds me of. The tang from the sour cream and cream cheese just cozies right up to the berries. Use very high-quality strawberry jam (not jelly) that tastes like the essence of freshly picked strawberries. Also, don't leave out the salt—it's critical for flavor balancing here.

YIELD • 2 SERVINGS

½ cup strawberry jam

¼ teaspoon salt

⅓ cup sour cream

3 ounces cream cheese

⅓ cup heavy cream

1 tablespoon powdered sugar

1 teaspoon rose water (optional)

Fresh strawberries, for garnish

Place the jam, salt, sour cream, and cream cheese in a blender (or food processor). Puree the mixture until it's smooth.

In a separate bowl, add the heavy cream and whip until soft peaks form. Add the powdered sugar and beat to combine.

Fold the two mixtures together and stir in the rose water, if using.

Divide the mousse between two serving bowls and chill them for 1 hour before serving with fresh strawberries.

Easiest Chocolate Pudding

This dessert has a super-fancy name. It's actually pots de crème. But I'll translate it for you: It's chocolate pudding that doesn't require any cooking at all. It's perfection. It sets entirely in the fridge. So, while you have to wait a few hours for everything to set, at least you don't have to turn on the oven.

Since this recipe uses a raw egg yolk, make sure your eggs come from a clean, reliable source.

YIELD · 2 SERVINGS

5 ounces semisweet chocolate chips

⅛ teaspoon salt

2 tablespoons granulated sugar

1 large egg yolk

½ teaspoon vanilla extract

¾ cup heavy whipping cream

¼ cup very hot prepared espresso, or ¼ cup very hot water + 1 teaspoon instant espresso powder

Whipped cream, for serving

Blood orange slices, for serving (optional)

In the bowl of a food processor, combine the chocolate chips, salt, and sugar. Pulse 10 to 15 times to break up the chocolate chips. The grittiness of the sugar will help this process. Add the egg yolk and vanilla. Pulse to combine.

Warm the cream in the microwave on low until warm to the touch, about 45 seconds.

While the processor is running, stream in the hot espresso and warm cream. Let the machine continue to run until the chocolate melts, and the mixture appears homogeneous.

Divide the mixture between two petite serving glasses.

Cover and chill in the fridge for at least 6 hours.

Serve with whipped cream and blood orange slices, if desired.

Mini Bread Puddings
with Brown Sugar Whiskey Caramel

I'm a newly converted bread pudding fan. I'm not sure what took me so long. Maybe it's because I never had bread pudding with a brown sugar whiskey caramel sauce until now.

YIELD · 6 MINI BREAD
PUDDINGS

3 tablespoons unsalted butter, divided

¼ cup pecan halves

½ cup milk

½ cup heavy whipping cream

¼ cup granulated sugar

½ teaspoon ground cinnamon

Pinch of freshly grated nutmeg

½ teaspoon vanilla extract

¼ teaspoon almond extract

1 large egg + 1 large egg yolk

2½ cups white bread cubes (from about 3 slices of bread)

FOR THE BROWN SUGAR WHISKEY CARAMEL SAUCE

¼ cup dark brown sugar

3 tablespoons heavy whipping cream

Splash of whiskey

Place 1 tablespoon of the butter in a small skillet and turn the heat to medium-low. Add the pecans when the butter melts, and toast gently until fragrant and beginning to darken in several places. Remove from the heat and pour into a bowl immediately to stop the cooking process.

Preheat the oven to 325°F and grease six cups of a muffin pan with oil or cooking spray.

Melt the remaining 2 tablespoons of butter and add to a medium bowl. Whisk in the milk, cream, granulated sugar, cinnamon, nutmeg, vanilla, and almond extract. Don't be tempted to skip the almond extract; it's pivotal here. If you're out, though, use an extra bump of vanilla in its place. Finally, stir in the egg and egg yolk.

Add the bread cubes, stir, and let sit for 5 minutes.

Divide the bread cube mixture equally among the prepared muffin cups, not worrying so much about the liquid. After all of the bread is divided, even out the amount of liquid between the cups—it should fill about three-fourths of the way in each cup.

Bake the bread puddings for 20 minutes.

After 20 minutes, scatter the pecans and any excess butter on top, and return the bread puddings to the oven for another 7 to 10 minutes.

Let the puddings cool in the pan for 10 minutes before removing with a knife.

Chai Pudding
with Gingersnap Crumbles

It's a bit hard for me to put words to my feelings for this recipe. Warm, spicy chai pudding—I couldn't dream up anything better.

   While this pudding is great served chilled like regular pudding, it really shines when served warm, especially over a slice of chocolate cake.

YIELD · 2 SERVINGS

½ cup granulated sugar

2 tablespoons cornstarch

⅛ teaspoon fine sea salt

1¼ cup milk

½ cup heavy cream

1 large egg yolk

½ teaspoon cinnamon

¼ teaspoon cardamom

¼ teaspoon ground cloves (or 1 whole clove in the milk mixture)

¼ teaspoon allspice

2 slices of fresh ginger, 1 inch thick, smashed

1 tablespoon unsalted butter

½ teaspoon vanilla extract

8 gingersnap cookies, crushed, for serving

In a medium glass bowl, combine the sugar, cornstarch, salt, and spices. Stir with a whisk to blend very well. (If you're using a whole clove instead of ground cloves, add it to the milk to steep while cooking, and then remove before serving.)

Slowly pour in ¼ cup of the cream and whisk vigorously to dissolve the sugar and cornstarch. Add the last of the cream slowly, still whisking.

Add the milk slowly and whisk very well to ensure all the dry ingredients are dissolved.

Pour the milk and cream mixture into a saucepan and add the smashed ginger slices.

Put the saucepan on the stove over medium heat. Bring the pudding to a simmer while constantly stirring with a wooden spoon. Be sure to scrape the sides and bottom of the saucepan during cooking.

Place the egg yolk in a separate small bowl and have it ready on the side.

When the pudding starts to gently simmer, turn the heat to low. Ladle a small amount (about 2 tablespoons) of the pudding into the bowl with the egg yolk and whisk very well. Repeat three times. Pour the egg yolk and pudding mixture back into the pan with the rest of the pudding.

Bring the pudding back to a gentle simmer and cook another one minute. Turn off the heat and stir in the butter and vanilla.

Remove the ginger slices (and whole clove, if used).

Pour the pudding into two small cups, cover with plastic wrap, and refrigerate at least 4 hours before serving. (If you don't like pudding skin, press the plastic wrap directly on the surface of the pudding before chilling.)

Before serving, remove the plastic wrap and top with the crushed gingersnap cookies.

Blender Chocolate Mousse for Two

Just four ingredients make this incredibly easy chocolate mousse recipe, and we absolutely cannot stop eating it. It's great for Valentine's Day, date night at home, or any other day that you need a rich chocolate fix.

YIELD · 2 SERVINGS

6 ounces 60 percent chocolate, chopped

⅔ cup heavy cream (divided use)

¼ cup hot espresso

1 large egg yolk

Whipped cream, for serving

Chocolate shavings, for serving

Chop the chocolate into very small pieces and add to a blender or small food processor. Pulse a few times to break up the chocolate even more.

Heat ⅓ cup of the heavy cream until steaming hot either in the microwave or in a small saucepan. Brew the espresso and reheat if not steaming hot.

Add the hot espresso, hot cream, and egg yolk to the blender with the chocolate mixture. Place the lid on to trap the steam so that the chocolate begins to melt for a minute or two.

Then blend until smooth, keeping the lid on the entire time so that the heat melts the chocolate.

If your chocolate mixture is not fully melted and is grainy or chunky after few minutes, you can put it in a glass measuring cup. Then, put the glass measuring cup in a bowl of very hot water; stir until everything melts. Set aside to cool.

Whip the remaining ⅓ cup of cold heavy cream until stiff peaks form.

Slowly fold in half of the chocolate mixture to the whipped cream, followed by the remaining chocolate and fold gently by hand until smooth.

Divide between two glasses, chill for one hour, and then serve with whipped cream and chocolate shavings.

INDEX

Page numbers in **bold** indicate an illustration.